Ivan Kushnir

Economy of China

Series "Economy in countries"

first published: 2019
last updated: 2021-01-26

Ivan Kushnir. Economy of China. Series "Economy in countries". - 2019. - 67 pages.

This book about the economy of China from the 1970s to the 2010s. Source data from UN Data.

Size. In the 2010s, the GDP of China was equal to $10.5 trillion per year; the value of agriculture was $886.2 billion; the value of industry was $3.7 trillion. Since the share in the world is greater than 10%, the country is classified as a global leader.

Productivity. In the 2010s, the GDP per capita was $7 491.3, the value of agriculture per capita was $631.9, the value of industry per capita was $2 626.2. Since the productivity is between the average of below average and the average, the economy is classified as developing.

Growth. In the 2010s, the growth of gross domestic product was 7.7%; the growth of agriculture was 3.8%; the growth of industry was 7.5%.

Structure. In the 2010s, the economy of China included: industry (35.1%), services (33.8%), trade (11.4%), agriculture (8.4%), construction (7.0%), and transportation (4.4%).

Exports and imports. In the 2010s, the exports were 10.8% higher than the imports, the net exports were equal to 2.1% of the GDP. The technological structure of exports are better than the structure of imports.

Consumption and reproduction. The attitude of reproduction to the consumption is better than the global average, so the share of GDP in the world will increase.

Series "Economy in countries": parallel.page.link/en

ISBN: 9781795027854

Contents

Part I. Size

	The 2010s
GDP	$10.5 trillion
The share in the world	13.5%
Share in Asia	38.4%
Share in Eastern Asia	58.1%

Chapter I. Gross domestic product

The China's GDP grew up from $156.3 billion per year in the 1970s to $10.5 trillion per year in the 2010s, that is by $10.3 trillion or 67.2 times. The change occurred at $4.9 trillion due to a 1.9-fold increase in prices, as also at $5.4 trillion due to a 23.5-fold increase in productivity, as well as at $83.5 billion due to the expansion in population. The average annual growth in GDP is 8.8%. The minimum value of GDP was in 1970 at $92.6 billion. The maximum value of GDP was in 2019 at $14.3 trillion.

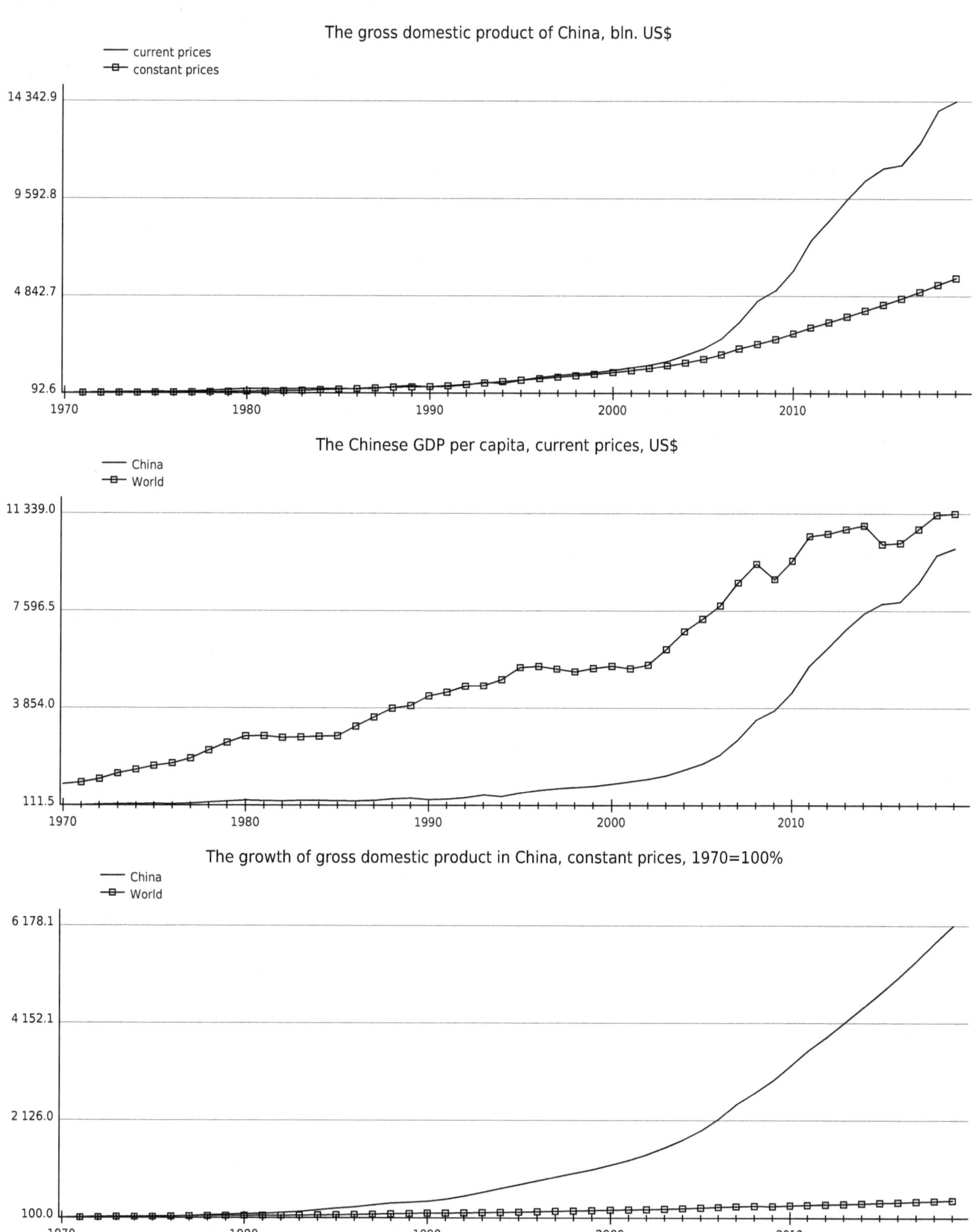

The 1970s

The China's gross domestic product was $156.3 billion per year in the 1970s, ranked 9th in the world. The share in the world was 2.4%, and 12.8% in Asia.

The GDP of China included: household expenditure (50.7%), capital formation (35.2%), and government expenditure (12.4%).

The Chinese gross domestic product per capita was $171.0 in the 1970s, ranked 167th in the world, and was on a par with Haiti ($174.3). The Chinese gross domestic product per capita was less than GDP per capita in the world ($1 620.8) in 9.5 times, and was less than GDP per capita in Asia ($525.2) in 3.1 times.

The growth of GDP in China was 6% in the 1970s, ranked 53rd in the world, and was on a par with the Philippines (6.0%), Jordan (6.0%), Egypt (6.1%). The growth of gross domestic product in China (6.0%) was greater than growth of gross domestic product in the world (4.1%), was greater than growth of gross domestic product in Asia (5.5%).

Comparison with neighbors. The GDP of China was greater than in India ($100.0 billion), in Republic of Korea ($27.2 billion), in Vietnam ($4.4 billion), and in Myanmar ($4.0 billion); but less than in the USSR ($649.4 billion) and in Japan ($558.0 billion). The Chinese GDP per capita was greater than in India ($162.0), in Myanmar ($130.3), and in Vietnam ($90.5); but less than in Japan ($5.0 thousand), in the USSR ($2.6 thousand), and in Republic of Korea ($778.5). The growth of GDP in China was greater than in the USSR (4.8%), in Vietnam (4.7%), in Japan (4.6%), in Myanmar (3.9%), and in India (2.6%); but less than in Republic of Korea (10.6%).

Comparison with leaders. The Chinese GDP was less than in the USA ($1.7 trillion), in the USSR ($649.4 billion), in Japan ($558.0 billion), in Germany ($484.2 billion), and in France ($333.2 billion). The Chinese gross domestic product per capita was less than in the USA ($7.8 thousand), in France ($6.2 thousand), in Germany ($6.1 thousand), in Japan ($5.0 thousand), and in the USSR ($2.6 thousand). The growth of gross domestic product in China was greater than in the USSR (4.8%), in Japan (4.6%), in France (3.9%), in the United States (3.5%), and in Germany (3.1%).

The 1980s

The China's GDP was $330.0 billion per year in the 1980s, ranked 9th in the world. The share in the world was 2.2%, and 9.5% in Asia.

The gross domestic product of China consisted of: household consumption expenditure (51.3%), capital formation (36.6%), and government expenditure (13.5%).

The GDP per capita in China was $307.7 in the 1980s, ranked 168th in the world, and was on a par with Malawi ($308.8), India ($310.5), Rwanda ($304.0). The China's gross domestic product per capita was less than GDP per capita in the world ($3 123.4) in 10.2 times, and was less than GDP per capita in Asia ($1 222.0) in 4.0 times.

The growth of gross domestic product in China was 9.7% in the 1980s, ranked 5th in the world. The growth of GDP in China (9.7%) was greater than growth of gross domestic product in the world (3.0%), was greater than growth of GDP in Asia (4.6%).

Comparison with neighbors. The gross domestic product of China was greater than in India ($241.0 billion), in South Korea ($121.5 billion), in Myanmar ($6.0 billion), and in Vietnam ($4.2 billion); but less than in Japan ($1.8 trillion) and in the USSR ($887.0 billion). The Chinese gross domestic product per capita was greater than in Myanmar ($161.0) and in Vietnam ($69.7); but less than in Japan ($15.0 thousand), in the USSR ($3.2 thousand), in South Korea ($3.0 thousand), and in India ($310.5). The growth of gross domestic product in China was greater than in Republic of Korea (8.8%), in India (5.7%), in Vietnam (4.7%), in the USSR (4.3%), in Japan (4.3%), and in Myanmar (1.5%).

Comparison with leaders. The China's gross domestic product was less than in the USA ($4.2 trillion), in Japan ($1.8 trillion), in Germany ($990.0 billion), in the USSR ($887.0 billion), and in France ($729.5 billion). The GDP per capita in China was less than in the USA ($17.4 thousand), in Japan ($15.0 thousand), in France ($12.9 thousand), in Germany ($12.7 thousand), and in the USSR ($3.2 thousand). The growth of gross domestic product in China was greater than in the USSR (4.3%), in Japan (4.3%), in the United States (3.1%), in France (2.3%), and in Germany (1.9%).

The 1990s

The gross domestic product of China was $716.7 billion per year in the 1990s, ranked 7th in the world. The share in the world was 2.5%, and 9.2% in Asia.

The gross domestic product of China included: household expenditure (46.0%), capital formation (37.8%), public expenditure (14.3%), and net export (2.4%).

The GDP per capita in China was $581.3 in the 1990s, ranked 164th in the world, and was on a par with Azerbaijan ($589.4). The Chinese GDP per capita was less than gross domestic product per capita in the world ($5 020.1) in 8.6 times, and was less than GDP per capita in Asia ($2 243.8) in 3.9 times.

The growth of gross domestic product in China was 10% in the 1990s, ranked 7th in the world, and was on a par with the Turks and Caicos Islands (9.9%), Eritrea (10.0%). The growth of GDP in China (10.0%) was greater than growth of GDP in the world (2.8%), was greater than growth of gross domestic product in Asia (4.7%).

Comparison with neighbors. The GDP of China was greater than in Republic of Korea ($445.3 billion), in Russia ($417.8 billion), in India ($361.1 billion), in Kazakhstan ($23.3 billion), in Vietnam ($18.2 billion), and in Myanmar ($7.9 billion); but less than in Japan ($4.3 trillion). The GDP per capita in China was greater than in India ($378.0), in Vietnam ($245.2), and in Myanmar ($181.0); but less than in Japan ($34.3 thousand), in South Korea ($9.9 thousand), in Russia ($2.8 thousand), and in Kazakhstan ($1 469.7). The growth of GDP in China was greater than in Vietnam (7.4%), in South Korea (7.2%), in Myanmar (6.5%), in India (5.7%), in Japan (1.5%), in Kazakhstan (-5.0%), and in Russia (-5.3%).

Comparison with leaders. The GDP of China was less than in the United States ($7.6 trillion), in Japan ($4.3 trillion), in Germany ($2.2 trillion), in France ($1.4 trillion), and in the UK ($1.3 trillion). The China's GDP per capita was less than in Japan ($34.3 thousand), in the United States ($28.7 thousand), in Germany ($27.0 thousand), in France ($24.1 thousand), and in the UK ($22.9 thousand). The growth of GDP in China was greater than in the United States (3.2%), in the UK (2.3%), in Germany (2.2%), in France (2.0%), and in Japan (1.5%).

The 2000s

The GDP of China was $2.6 trillion per year in the 2000s, ranked 4th in the world. The share in the world was 5.6%, and 20.6% in Asia.

The gross domestic product of China included: capital formation (41.9%), household expenditure (39.2%), government consumption expenditure (14.0%), and net export (5.4%).

The Chinese gross domestic product per capita was $1 954.1 in the 2000s, ranked 137th in the world, and was on a par with Vanuatu ($1 953.5), Armenia ($1 915.3). The Chinese GDP per capita was less than gross domestic product per capita in the world ($7 176.3) in 3.7 times, and was less than gross domestic product per capita in Asia ($3 180.5) by 38.6%.

The growth of gross domestic product in China was 10.3% in the 2000s, ranked 5th in the world. The growth of GDP in China (10.3%) was greater than growth of GDP in the world (3.0%), was greater than growth of GDP in Asia (5.2%).

Comparison with neighbors. The GDP of China was greater than in Republic of Korea ($839.9 billion), in India ($831.2 billion), in Russia ($794.5 billion), in Kazakhstan ($63.1 billion), in Vietnam ($59.5 billion), and in Myanmar ($16.9 billion); but less than in Japan ($4.7 trillion). The gross domestic product per capita in China was greater than in India ($730.3), in Vietnam ($712.4), and in Myanmar ($346.6); but less than in Japan ($36.4 thousand), in Republic of Korea ($17.3 thousand), in Russia ($5.5 thousand), and in Kazakhstan ($4.1 thousand). The growth of GDP in China was greater than in Kazakhstan (8.5%), in Vietnam (6.8%), in India (6.3%), in Russia (5.4%), in Republic of Korea (4.9%), and in Japan (0.50%); but less than in Myanmar (12.2%).

Comparison with leaders. The Chinese gross domestic product was greater than in the United Kingdom ($2.3 trillion) and in France ($2.1 trillion); but less than in the USA ($12.6 trillion), in Japan ($4.7 trillion), and in Germany ($2.8 trillion). The Chinese gross domestic product per capita was less than in the United States ($42.8 thousand), in the United Kingdom ($38.4 thousand), in Japan ($36.4 thousand), in Germany ($34.0 thousand), and in France ($33.4 thousand). The growth of GDP in China was greater than in the United States (1.9%), in the United Kingdom (1.7%), in France (1.4%), in Germany (0.73%), and in Japan (0.50%).

The 2010s

The China's GDP was $10.5 trillion per year in the 2010s, ranked 2nd in the world. The share in the world was 13.5%, and 38.4% in Asia.

The GDP of China consisted of: capital formation (44.5%), household expenditure (37.4%), government consumption expenditure (16.0%), and net export (2.1%).

The gross domestic product per capita in China was $7 491.3 in the 2010s, ranked 95th in the world, and was on a par with Cuba ($7.5

thousand), Botswana ($7.4 thousand), Dominica ($7.4 thousand). The Chinese gross domestic product per capita was less than GDP per capita in the world ($10 603.1) by 29.3%, and was greater than gross domestic product per capita in Asia ($6 207.1) by 20.7%.

The growth of gross domestic product in China was 7.7% in the 2010s, ranked 8th in the world, and was on a par with Mongolia (7.6%). The growth of gross domestic product in China (7.7%) was greater than growth of GDP in the world (3.1%), was greater than growth of GDP in Asia (5.2%).

Comparison with neighbors. The China's gross domestic product was 2.0 times higher than in Japan ($5.2 trillion), 4.8 times higher than in India ($2.2 trillion), 5.9 times higher than in Russia ($1.8 trillion), 7.2 times higher than in South Korea ($1.4 trillion), 55.5 times higher than in Vietnam ($189.4 billion), 56.6 times higher than in Kazakhstan ($185.6 billion), and 160.1 times higher than in Myanmar ($65.6 billion). The Chinese GDP per capita was 3.6 times higher than in Vietnam ($2.1 thousand), 4.4 times higher than in India ($1 696.8), and 6.0 times higher than in Myanmar ($1 252.3); but 5.5 times lower than in Japan ($40.9 thousand), 3.8 times lower than in Republic of Korea ($28.7 thousand), 38.9% lower than in Russia ($12.3 thousand), and 29.7% lower than in Kazakhstan ($10.7 thousand). The growth of gross domestic product in China was greater than in India (6.7%), in Myanmar (6.6%), in Vietnam (6.3%), in Kazakhstan (4.5%), in South Korea (3.3%), in Russia (1.9%), and in Japan (1.3%).

Comparison with leaders. The Chinese GDP was 2.0 times higher than in Japan ($5.2 trillion), 2.9 times higher than in Germany ($3.7 trillion), 3.8 times higher than in the UK ($2.8 trillion), and 3.9 times higher than in France ($2.7 trillion); but 41.5% lower than in the USA ($18.0 trillion). The gross domestic product per capita in China was 7.5 times lower than in the United States ($56.2 thousand), 6.0 times lower than in Germany ($44.7 thousand), 5.6 times lower than in the United Kingdom ($42.2 thousand), 5.5 times lower than in Japan ($40.9 thousand), and 5.4 times lower than in France ($40.5 thousand). The growth of gross domestic product in China was greater than in the United States (2.3%), in Germany (1.9%), in the United Kingdom (1.8%), in France (1.4%), and in Japan (1.3%).

Chapter II. Value added

The value added of China enlarged from $156.3 billion per year in the 1970s to $10.5 trillion per year in the 2010s, that is by $10.3 trillion or 67.2 times. The change occurred at $5.7 trillion due to a 2.2-fold increase in prices, as also at $4.6 trillion due to a 20.2-fold increase in productivity, as well as at $83.5 billion due to the increase in population. The average annual growth in value added is 8.3%. The minimum value of value added was in 1970 at $92.6 billion. The maximum value of value added was in 2019 at $14.3 trillion.

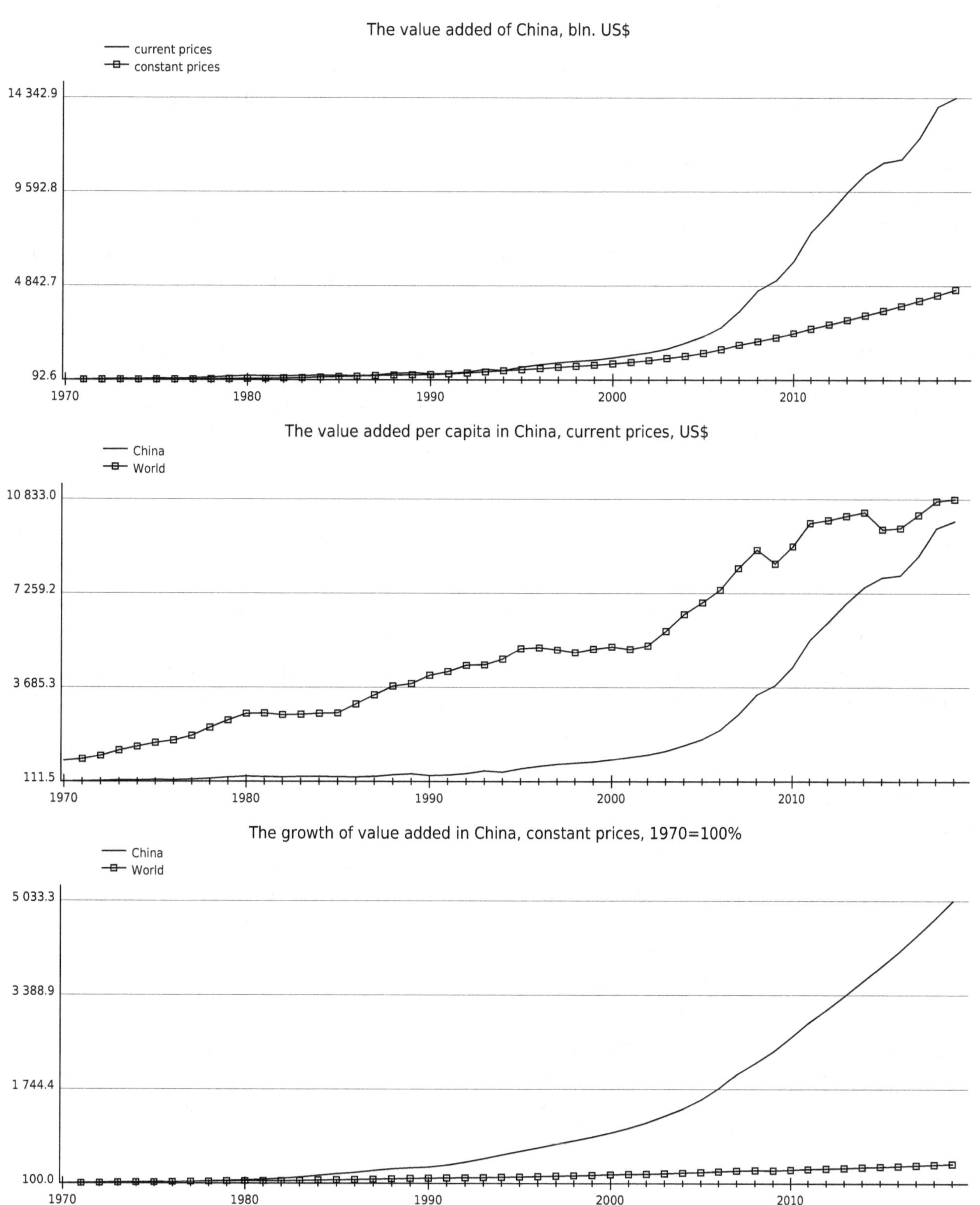

The 1970s

The value added of China was $156.3 billion per year in the 1970s, ranked 8th in the world, and was on a par with Canada ($155.4 billion). The share in the world was 2.5%, and 13.2% in Asia.

The total value added of China included: industry (41.1%), agriculture (31.7%), services (11.4%), trade (7.1%), transportation (4.8%), and construction (3.9%).

The China's value added per capita was $171.0 in the 1970s, ranked 168th in the world, and was on a par with Chad ($168.3). The value added per capita in China was less than value added per capita in the world ($1 564.4) in 9.1 times, and was less than value added per capita in Asia ($508.3) in 3.0 times.

The growth of value added in China was 4.7% in the 1970s, ranked 82nd in the world, and was on a par with Vietnam (4.7%), Turkey (4.7%), Haiti (4.7%). The growth of value added in China (4.7%) was greater than growth of value added in the world (3.9%), was less than growth of value added in Asia (5.5%).

Comparison with neighbors. The value added of China was greater than in India ($90.5 billion), in Republic of Korea ($24.5 billion), in Vietnam ($4.8 billion), and in Myanmar ($3.8 billion); but less than in the USSR ($649.4 billion) and in Japan ($545.3 billion). The China's value added per capita was greater than in India ($146.6), in Myanmar ($123.9), and in Vietnam ($99.7); but less than in Japan ($4.9 thousand), in the USSR ($2.6 thousand), and in Republic of Korea ($701.6). The growth of value added in China was greater than in Vietnam (4.7%), in Myanmar (3.7%), and in India (2.4%); but less than in South Korea (9.0%), in Japan (4.9%), and in the USSR (4.8%).

Comparison with leaders. The Chinese value added was less than in the United States ($1.7 trillion), in the USSR ($649.4 billion), in Japan ($545.3 billion), in Germany ($444.9 billion), and in France ($297.3 billion). The China's value added per capita was less than in the United States ($7.8 thousand), in Germany ($5.7 thousand), in France ($5.5 thousand), in Japan ($4.9 thousand), and in the USSR ($2.6 thousand). The growth of value added in China was greater than in France (3.7%), in Germany (3.1%), and in the United States (2.9%); but less than in Japan (4.9%) and in the USSR (4.8%).

The 1980s

The value added of China was $330.0 billion per year in the 1980s, ranked 9th in the world. The share in the world was 2.3%, and 9.8% in Asia.

The total value added of China consisted of: industry (39.5%), agriculture (28.8%), services (14.3%), trade (8.1%), construction (4.7%), and transportation (4.6%).

The value added per capita in China was $307.7 in the 1980s, ranked 165th in the world, and was on a par with Benin ($308.5), Togo ($312.6). The Chinese value added per capita was less than value added per capita in the world ($3 029.9) in 9.8 times, and was less than value added per capita in Asia ($1 191.9) in 3.9 times.

The growth of value added in China was 9.4% in the 1980s, ranked 8th in the world, and was on a par with Mongolia (9.4%), Bhutan (9.5%). The growth of value added in China (9.4%) was greater than growth of value added in the world (2.9%), was greater than growth of value added in Asia (4.3%).

Comparison with neighbors. The China's value added was greater than in India ($212.0 billion), in South Korea ($109.4 billion), in Myanmar ($6.1 billion), and in Vietnam ($4.6 billion); but less than in Japan ($1.8 trillion) and in the USSR ($887.0 billion). The value added per capita in China was greater than in India ($273.2), in Myanmar ($162.7), and in Vietnam ($76.8); but less than in Japan ($14.8 thousand), in the USSR ($3.2 thousand), and in South Korea ($2.7 thousand). The growth of value added in China was greater than in South Korea (8.4%), in India (5.8%), in Vietnam (4.8%), in the USSR (4.3%), in Japan (4.2%), and in Myanmar (1.5%).

Comparison with leaders. The Chinese value added was less than in the United States ($4.2 trillion), in Japan ($1.8 trillion), in Germany ($907.0 billion), in the USSR ($887.0 billion), and in France ($650.9 billion). The Chinese value added per capita was less than in the USA ($17.4 thousand), in Japan ($14.8 thousand), in Germany ($11.6 thousand), in France ($11.5 thousand), and in the USSR ($3.2 thousand). The growth of value added in China was greater than in the USSR (4.3%), in Japan (4.2%), in the USA (2.8%), in France (2.2%), and in Germany (2.0%).

The 1990s

The Chinese value added was $716.7 billion per year in the 1990s, ranked 7th in the world, and was on a par with Eastern Europe ($726.1 billion). The share in the world was 2.6%, and 9.4% in Asia.

The total value added of China consisted of: industry (39.9%), agriculture (19.4%), services (19.3%), trade (10.0%), construction (5.8%), and transportation (5.7%).

The Chinese value added per capita was $581.3 in the 1990s, ranked 162nd in the world, and was on a par with Mongolia ($582.4), Moldova ($579.0), Sri Lanka ($578.6). The Chinese value added per capita was less than value added per capita in the world ($4 799.9) in 8.3 times, and was less than value added per capita in Asia ($2 197.3) in 3.8 times.

The growth of value added in China was 9.4% in the 1990s, ranked 8th in the world. The growth of value added in China (9.4%) was greater than growth of value added in the world (2.7%), was greater than growth of value added in Asia (4.6%).

Comparison with neighbors. The value added of China was greater than in South Korea ($404.9 billion), in Russia ($392.4 billion), in India ($321.6 billion), in Kazakhstan ($24.0 billion), in Vietnam ($20.0 billion), and in Myanmar ($8.0 billion); but less than in Japan ($4.3 trillion). The China's value added per capita was greater than in India ($336.7), in Vietnam ($270.0), and in Myanmar ($182.0); but less than in Japan ($34.2 thousand), in South Korea ($9.0 thousand), in Russia ($2.7 thousand), and in Kazakhstan ($1 512.9). The growth of value added in China was greater than in Vietnam (8.2%), in Republic of Korea (6.9%), in Myanmar (6.3%), in India (5.6%), in Japan (1.8%), in Russia (-4.8%), and in Kazakhstan (-5.1%).

Comparison with leaders. The value added of China was less than in the USA ($7.6 trillion), in Japan ($4.3 trillion), in Germany ($2.0 trillion), in France ($1.3 trillion), and in the UK ($1.2 trillion). The value added per capita in China was less than in Japan ($34.2 thousand), in the USA ($28.6 thousand), in Germany ($24.5 thousand), in France ($21.6 thousand), and in the United Kingdom ($21.4 thousand). The growth of value added in China was greater than in the United States (2.8%), in the UK (2.4%), in Germany (2.1%), in France (1.8%), and in Japan (1.8%).

The 2000s

The China's value added was $2.6 trillion per year in the 2000s, ranked 3rd in the world. The share in the world was 5.8%, and 21.1% in Asia.

The total value added of China consisted of: industry (40.7%), services (26.5%), agriculture (11.5%), trade (10.1%), construction (5.8%), and transportation (5.4%).

The China's value added per capita was $1 954.1 in the 2000s, ranked 134th in the world, and was on a par with Northern Africa ($1 947.7), Melanesia ($1 963.3), Guatemala ($1 917.0). The China's value added per capita was less than value added per capita in the world ($6 818.0) in 3.5 times, and was less than value added per capita in Asia ($3 111.3) by 37.2%.

The growth of value added in China was 10.2% in the 2000s, ranked 6th in the world. The growth of value added in China (10.2%) was greater than growth of value added in the world (2.9%), was greater than growth of value added in Asia (5.1%).

Comparison with neighbors. The Chinese value added was greater than in India ($760.7 billion), in South Korea ($760.6 billion), in Russia ($685.9 billion), in Kazakhstan ($61.1 billion), in Vietnam ($60.8 billion), and in Myanmar ($16.5 billion); but less than in Japan ($4.7 trillion). The Chinese value added per capita was greater than in Vietnam ($728.6), in India ($668.3), and in Myanmar ($339.3); but less than in Japan ($36.4 thousand), in South Korea ($15.7 thousand), in Russia ($4.8 thousand), and in Kazakhstan ($4.0 thousand). The growth of value added in China was greater than in Kazakhstan (8.6%), in Vietnam (6.5%), in India (6.2%), in Russia (5.0%), in Republic of Korea (4.8%), and in Japan (0.27%); but less than in Myanmar (12.4%).

Comparison with leaders. The value added of China was greater than in Germany ($2.5 trillion), in the UK ($2.1 trillion), and in France ($1.9 trillion); but less than in the USA ($12.6 trillion) and in Japan ($4.7 trillion). The China's value added per capita was less than in the United States ($42.8 thousand), in Japan ($36.4 thousand), in the UK ($34.6 thousand), in Germany ($30.7 thousand), and in France ($30.0 thousand). The growth of value added in China was greater than in the United States (1.7%), in the United Kingdom (1.7%), in France (1.4%), in Germany (0.65%), and in Japan (0.27%).

The 2010s

The value added of China was $10.5 trillion per year in the 2010s, ranked 2nd in the world. The share in the world was 14.2%, and 39.3% in Asia.

The total value added of China consisted of: industry (35.1%), services (33.8%), trade (11.4%), agriculture (8.4%), construction (7.0%), and transportation (4.4%).

The value added per capita in China was $7 491.3 in the 2010s, ranked 92nd in the world, and was on a par with Cuba ($7.4 thousand), Grenada ($7.6 thousand). The China's value added per capita was less than value added per capita in the world ($10 094.6) by 25.8%, and was greater than value added per capita in Asia ($6 065.5) by 23.5%.

The growth of value added in China was 7.7% in the 2010s, ranked 8th in the world. The growth of value added in China (7.7%) was greater than growth of value added in the world (3.1%), was greater than growth of value added in Asia (5.3%).

Comparison with neighbors. The value added of China was 2.0 times higher than in Japan ($5.2 trillion), 5.2 times higher than in India ($2.0 trillion), 6.7 times higher than in Russia ($1.6 trillion), 7.9 times higher than in Republic of Korea ($1.3 trillion), 60.8 times higher than in Kazakhstan ($172.9 billion), 61.8 times higher than in Vietnam ($170.0 billion), and 161.9 times higher than in Myanmar ($64.9 billion). The value added per capita in China was 4.1 times higher than in Vietnam ($1 843.5), 4.8 times higher than in India ($1 552.2), and 6.1 times higher than in Myanmar ($1 238.2); but 5.4 times lower than in Japan ($40.7 thousand), 3.5 times lower than in South Korea ($26.2 thousand), 30.6% lower than in Russia ($10.8 thousand), and 24.5% lower than in Kazakhstan ($9.9 thousand). The growth of value added in China was greater than in Myanmar (6.9%), in India (6.8%), in Vietnam (5.0%), in Kazakhstan (4.5%), in South Korea (3.3%), in Russia (1.7%), and in Japan (1.3%).

Comparison with leaders. The Chinese value added was 2.0 times higher than in Japan ($5.2 trillion), 3.2 times higher than in Germany ($3.3 trillion), 4.3 times higher than in the United Kingdom ($2.5 trillion), and 4.4 times higher than in France ($2.4 trillion); but 41.5% lower than in the USA ($18.0 trillion). The Chinese value added per capita was 7.5 times lower than in the United States ($56.2 thousand), 5.4 times lower than in Japan ($40.7 thousand), 5.4 times lower than in Germany ($40.3 thousand), 5.0 times lower than in the UK ($37.7 thousand), and 4.8 times lower than in France ($36.2 thousand). The growth of value added in China was greater than in the USA (2.2%), in Germany (1.9%), in the United Kingdom (1.8%), in France (1.3%), and in Japan (1.3%).

Chapter III. Gross national income

The China's gross national income grew up from $167.9 billion per year in the 1970s to $10.5 trillion per year in the 2010s, that is by $10.3 trillion or 62.4 times. The change occurred at $4.9 trillion due to a 1.9-fold increase in prices, as also at $5.4 trillion due to a 21.8-fold increase in productivity, as well as at $89.7 billion due to the increase in population. The average annual growth in gross national income is 8.6%. The minimum value of gross national income was in 1970 at $99.6 billion. The maximum value of GNI was in 2019 at $14.3 trillion.

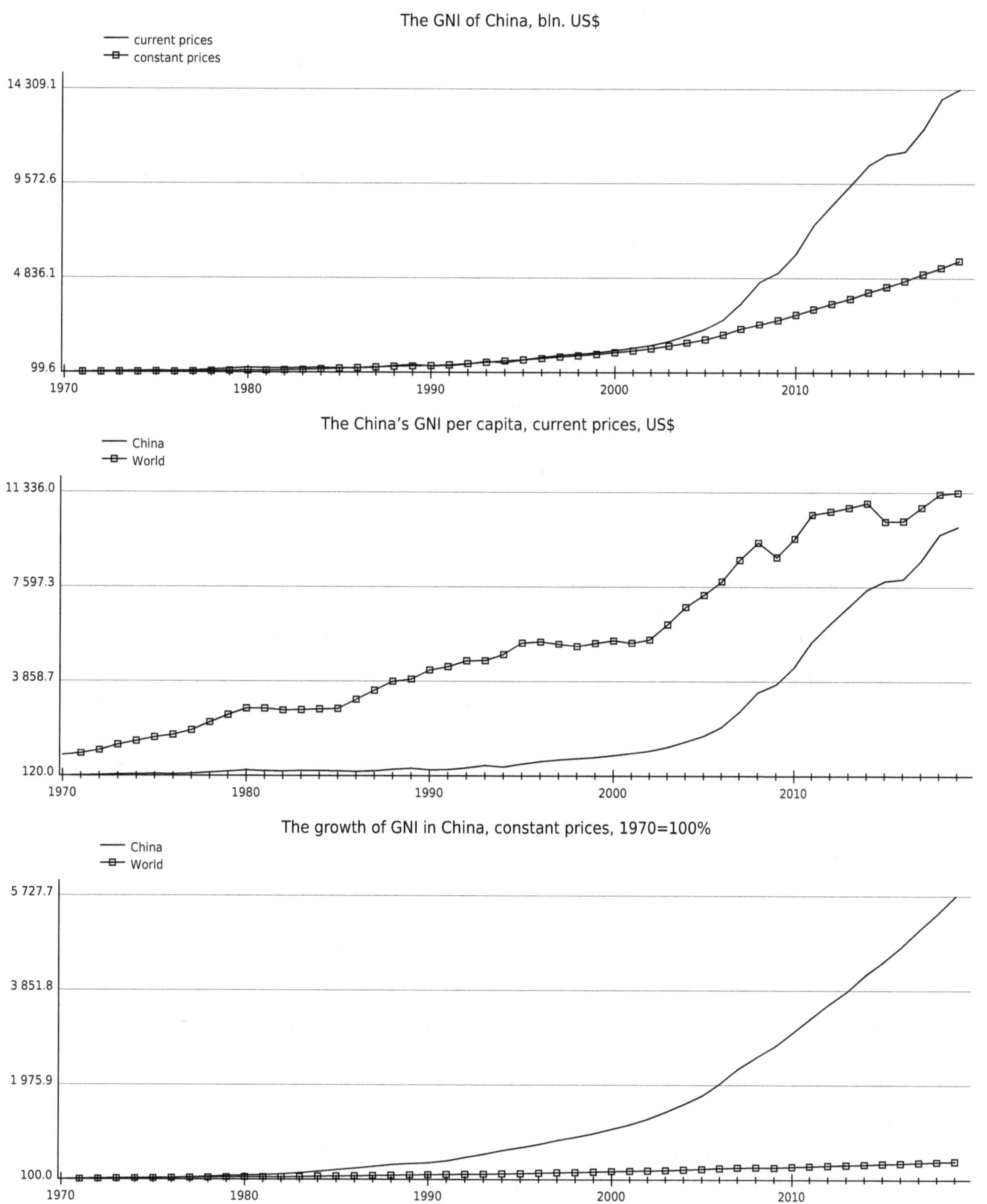

The 1970s

The gross national income of China was $167.9 billion per year in the 1970s, ranked 8th in the world, and was on a par with Western Asia ($168.6 billion). The share in the world was 2.6%, and 13.7% in Asia.

The GNI per capita in China was $183.6 in the 1970s, ranked 167th in the world, and was on a par with Benin ($183.6). The gross national income per capita in China was less than GNI per capita in the world ($1 624.3) in 8.8 times, and was less than GNI per capita in Asia ($529.4) in 2.9 times.

The growth of GNI in China was 6% in the 1970s, ranked 54th in the world, and was on a par with Poland (5.9%). The growth of GNI in China (6.0%) was greater than growth of GNI in the world (4.1%), was greater than growth of gross national income in Asia (5.5%).

Comparison with neighbors. The GNI of China was greater than in India ($99.7 billion), in South Korea ($27.2 billion), in Vietnam ($4.3 billion), and in Myanmar ($3.7 billion); but less than in the USSR ($649.4 billion) and in Japan ($558.5 billion). The GNI per capita in China was greater than in India ($161.6), in Myanmar ($122.7), and in Vietnam ($88.9); but less than in Japan ($5.0 thousand), in the USSR ($2.6 thousand), and in Republic of Korea ($778.4). The growth of GNI in China was greater than in the USSR (4.8%), in Japan (4.7%), in Vietnam (4.7%), and in India (2.7%); but less than in South Korea (10.3%) and in Myanmar (6.4%).

Comparison with leaders. The Chinese GNI was less than in the United States ($1.7 trillion), in the USSR ($649.4 billion), in Japan ($558.5 billion), in Germany ($486.2 billion), and in France ($334.3 billion). The China's gross national income per capita was less than in the USA ($7.8 thousand), in France ($6.2 thousand), in Germany ($6.2 thousand), in Japan ($5.0 thousand), and in the USSR ($2.6 thousand). The growth of GNI in China was greater than in the USSR (4.8%), in Japan (4.7%), in France (3.9%), in the USA (3.5%), and in Germany (3.0%).

The 1980s

The China's GNI was $347.6 billion per year in the 1980s, ranked 9th in the world. The share in the world was 2.3%, and 9.9% in Asia.

The Chinese GNI per capita was $324.1 in the 1980s, ranked 164th in the world. The GNI per capita in China was less than GNI per capita in the world ($3 117.1) in 9.6 times, and was less than GNI per capita in Asia ($1 233.8) in 3.8 times.

The growth of gross national income in China was 9.4% in the 1980s, ranked 6th in the world. The growth of GNI in China (9.4%) was greater than growth of gross national income in the world (3.0%), was greater than growth of gross national income in Asia (4.6%).

Comparison with neighbors. The Chinese GNI was greater than in India ($239.6 billion), in Republic of Korea ($120.1 billion), in Myanmar ($6.0 billion), and in Vietnam ($4.1 billion); but less than in Japan ($1.8 trillion) and in the USSR ($887.0 billion). The Chinese gross national income per capita was greater than in India ($308.7), in Myanmar ($160.7), and in Vietnam ($68.5); but less than in Japan ($15.0 thousand), in the USSR ($3.2 thousand), and in Republic of Korea ($3.0 thousand). The growth of GNI in China was greater than in South Korea (8.8%), in India (5.5%), in Vietnam (4.7%), in Japan (4.4%), in the USSR (4.3%), and in Myanmar (1.5%).

Comparison with leaders. The GNI of China was less than in the United States ($4.2 trillion), in Japan ($1.8 trillion), in Germany ($996.5 billion), in the USSR ($887.0 billion), and in France ($732.1 billion). The Chinese gross national income per capita was less than in the United States ($17.4 thousand), in Japan ($15.0 thousand), in France ($13.0 thousand), in Germany ($12.8 thousand), and in the USSR ($3.2 thousand). The growth of gross national income in China was greater than in Japan (4.4%), in the USSR (4.3%), in the USA (3.1%), in France (2.3%), and in Germany (2.0%).

The 1990s

The China's gross national income was $721.1 billion per year in the 1990s, ranked 7th in the world. The share in the world was 2.5%, and 9.2% in Asia.

The China's gross national income per capita was $584.9 in the 1990s, ranked 165th in the world, and was on a par with Azerbaijan ($591.8). The GNI per capita in China was less than gross national income per capita in the world ($4 991.4) in 8.5 times, and was less than gross national income per capita in Asia ($2 257.5) in 3.9 times.

The growth of GNI in China was 9.3% in the 1990s, ranked 7th in the world. The growth of gross national income in China (9.3%) was greater than growth of GNI in the world (2.8%), was greater than growth of GNI in Asia (4.6%).

Comparison with neighbors. The Chinese gross national income was greater than in Republic of Korea ($443.3 billion), in Russia

($411.1 billion), in India ($357.1 billion), in Kazakhstan ($23.1 billion), in Vietnam ($17.8 billion), and in Myanmar ($7.9 billion); but less than in Japan ($4.4 trillion). The China's gross national income per capita was greater than in India ($373.8), in Vietnam ($240.0), and in Myanmar ($180.2); but less than in Japan ($34.7 thousand), in Republic of Korea ($9.8 thousand), in Russia ($2.8 thousand), and in Kazakhstan ($1 459.2). The growth of GNI in China was greater than in Vietnam (7.4%), in South Korea (7.1%), in Myanmar (6.2%), in India (5.8%), in Japan (1.5%), in Kazakhstan (-5.3%), and in Russia (-5.7%).

Comparison with leaders. The China's gross national income was less than in the USA ($7.5 trillion), in Japan ($4.4 trillion), in Germany ($2.2 trillion), in France ($1.4 trillion), and in the United Kingdom ($1.3 trillion). The China's GNI per capita was less than in Japan ($34.7 thousand), in the United States ($28.5 thousand), in Germany ($27.0 thousand), in France ($24.3 thousand), and in the United Kingdom ($23.0 thousand). The growth of gross national income in China was greater than in the USA (3.4%), in France (2.2%), in the UK (2.0%), in Germany (2.0%), and in Japan (1.5%).

The 2000s

The Chinese gross national income was $2.6 trillion per year in the 2000s, ranked 4th in the world. The share in the world was 5.6%, and 20.5% in Asia.

The GNI per capita in China was $1 950.5 in the 2000s, ranked 137th in the world, and was on a par with Armenia ($1 955.0), Northern Africa ($1 995.7). The China's gross national income per capita was less than gross national income per capita in the world ($7 165.2) in 3.7 times, and was less than GNI per capita in Asia ($3 199.2) by 39.0%.

The growth of gross national income in China was 10.4% in the 2000s, ranked 6th in the world. The growth of GNI in China (10.4%) was greater than growth of gross national income in the world (3.0%), was greater than growth of GNI in Asia (5.3%).

Comparison with neighbors. The GNI of China was greater than in Republic of Korea ($837.1 billion), in India ($825.7 billion), in Russia ($771.8 billion), in Vietnam ($57.5 billion), in Kazakhstan ($56.3 billion), and in Myanmar ($16.4 billion); but less than in Japan ($4.8 trillion). The gross national income per capita in China was greater than in India ($725.4), in Vietnam ($689.4), and in Myanmar ($337.3); but less than in Japan ($37.1 thousand), in Republic of Korea ($17.3 thousand), in Russia ($5.3 thousand), and in Kazakhstan ($3.7 thousand). The growth of gross national income in China was greater than in Kazakhstan (7.6%), in Vietnam (6.6%), in India (6.3%), in Russia (5.5%), in South Korea (5.0%), and in Japan (0.62%); but less than in Myanmar (12.2%).

Comparison with leaders. The GNI of China was greater than in the United Kingdom ($2.3 trillion) and in France ($2.1 trillion); but less than in the United States ($12.7 trillion), in Japan ($4.8 trillion), and in Germany ($2.8 trillion). The gross national income per capita in China was less than in the USA ($43.2 thousand), in the UK ($38.5 thousand), in Japan ($37.1 thousand), in Germany ($34.2 thousand), and in France ($34.0 thousand). The growth of gross national income in China was greater than in the United States (1.8%), in the UK (1.7%), in France (1.5%), in Germany (1.0%), and in Japan (0.62%).

The 2010s

The China's gross national income was $10.5 trillion per year in the 2010s, ranked 2nd in the world. The share in the world was 13.4%, and 38.1% in Asia.

The China's gross national income per capita was $7 463.8 in the 2010s, ranked 94th in the world, and was on a par with Montenegro ($7.5 thousand), Cuba ($7.4 thousand). The Chinese gross national income per capita was less than gross national income per capita in the world ($10 611.7) by 29.7%, and was greater than gross national income per capita in Asia ($6 227.9) by 19.8%.

The growth of gross national income in China was 7.7% in the 2010s, ranked 8th in the world. The growth of gross national income in China (7.7%) was greater than growth of GNI in the world (3.1%), was greater than growth of gross national income in Asia (5.2%).

Comparison with neighbors. The China's gross national income was 93.9% higher than in Japan ($5.4 trillion), 4.8 times higher than in India ($2.2 trillion), 6.1 times higher than in Russia ($1.7 trillion), 7.2 times higher than in Republic of Korea ($1.5 trillion), 58.5 times higher than in Vietnam ($179.1 billion), 63.8 times higher than in Kazakhstan ($164.0 billion), and 162.8 times higher than in Myanmar ($64.3 billion). The Chinese GNI per capita was 3.8 times higher than in Vietnam ($1 942.0), 4.4 times higher than in India ($1 677.9), and 6.1 times higher than in Myanmar ($1 227.1); but 5.7 times lower than in Japan ($42.2 thousand), 3.9 times lower than in Republic of Korea ($28.8 thousand), 37.3% lower than in Russia ($11.9 thousand), and 20.7% lower than in Kazakhstan ($9.4 thousand). The growth of gross national income in China was greater than in India (6.6%), in Myanmar (6.5%), in Vietnam (6.0%), in Kazakhstan (4.2%), in Republic of Korea (3.4%), in Russia (1.9%), and in Japan (1.4%).

Comparison with leaders. The gross national income of China was 93.9% higher than in Japan ($5.4 trillion), 2.8 times higher than in Germany ($3.7 trillion), 3.8 times higher than in France ($2.7 trillion), and 3.8 times higher than in the UK ($2.7 trillion); but 42.8% lower than in the USA ($18.3 trillion). The gross national income per capita in China was 7.7 times lower than in the United States ($57.3 thousand), 6.1 times lower than in Germany ($45.8 thousand), 5.7 times lower than in Japan ($42.2 thousand), 5.6 times lower than in the UK ($41.6 thousand), and 5.5 times lower than in France ($41.4 thousand). The growth of GNI in China was greater than in the USA (2.5%), in Germany (2.0%), in the United Kingdom (1.7%), in Japan (1.4%), and in France (1.4%).

Part II. Structure

	The 2010s
agriculture	8.4%
industry	35.1%
construction	7.0%
trade	11.4%
transportation	4.4%
services	33.8%

Chapter IV. Agriculture

Agriculture, hunting, forestry, fishing (ISIC A-B)

The China's agriculture enlarged from $49.5 billion per year in the 1970s to $886.2 billion per year in the 2010s, that is by $836.7 billion or 17.9 times. The change occurred at $629.2 billion due to a 3.4-fold increase in prices, as also at $181.0 billion due to a 3.4-fold increase in productivity, as well as at $26.5 billion due to the growing in population. The average annual growth in agriculture is 4.0%. The minimum value of agriculture was in 1970 at $32.5 billion. The maximum value of agriculture was in 2019 at $1.1 trillion.

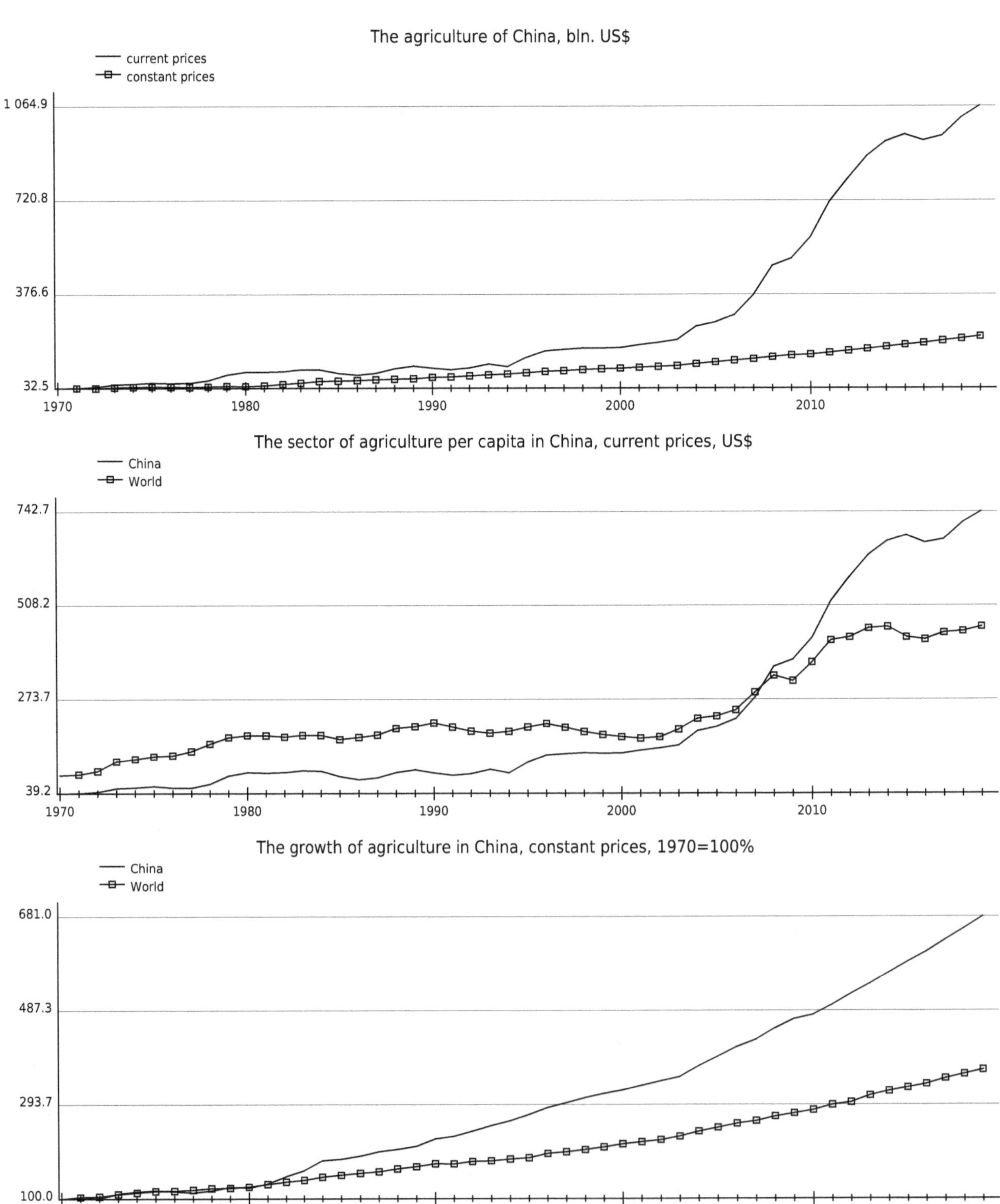

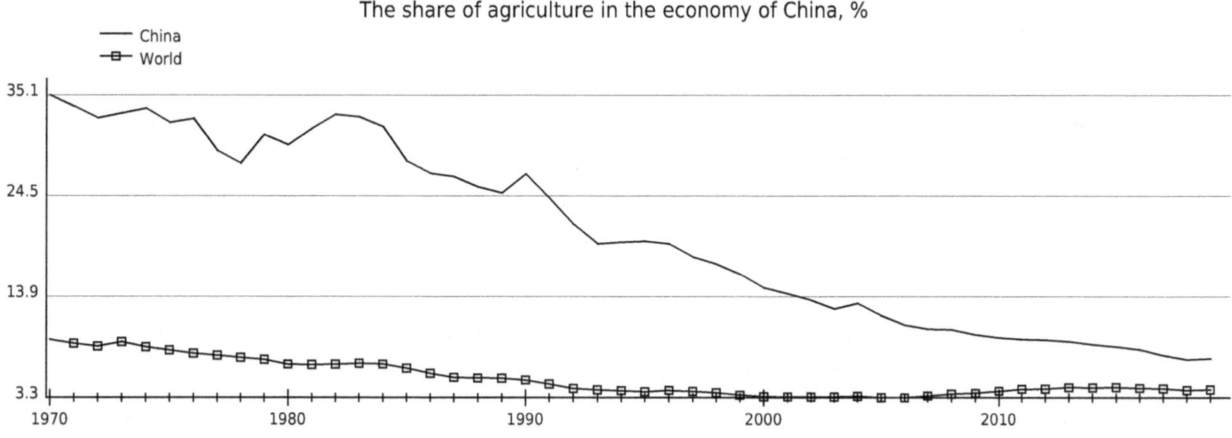

The 1970s

The value of agriculture in China was \$49.5 billion per year in the 1970s, ranked 2nd in the world, and was on a par with Northern America (\$49.5 billion). The share in the world was 9.6%, and 27.8% in Asia.

The share of agriculture in the economy of China was 31.7% in the 1970s, ranked 36th in the world, and was on a par with Vanuatu (31.6%), the CAR (31.9%).

The sector of agriculture per capita in China was \$54.2 in the 1970s, ranked 154th in the world, and was on a par with Liberia (\$54.3), Chad (\$54.4), Ethiopia (\$54.8). The Chinese agriculture per capita was less than agriculture per capita in the world (\$127.6) in 2.4 times, and was less than agriculture per capita in Asia (\$76.7) by 29.4%.

The growth of agriculture in China was 2.4% in the 1970s, ranked 101st in the world, and was on a par with Algeria (2.4%), Oceania (2.4%), Egypt (2.4%). The growth of agriculture in China (2.4%) was greater than growth of agriculture in the world (2.2%), was greater than growth of agriculture in Asia (2.0%).

Comparison with neighbors. The agriculture of China was greater than in India (\$36.0 billion), in Japan (\$25.8 billion), in Republic of Korea (\$5.9 billion), in Vietnam (\$1.9 billion), and in Myanmar (\$1.7 billion); but less than in the USSR (\$88.7 billion). The China's agriculture per capita was greater than in Vietnam (\$38.7); but less than in the USSR (\$351.8), in Japan (\$231.3), in Republic of Korea (\$170.0), in India (\$58.3), and in Myanmar (\$55.6). The growth of agriculture in China was greater than in Japan (0.52%) and in India (0.30%); but less than in the USSR (7.0%), in Vietnam (4.7%), in Republic of Korea (4.3%), and in Myanmar (3.9%).

Comparison with leaders. The value added of agriculture in China was greater than in the USA (\$42.6 billion), in India (\$36.0 billion), in Japan (\$25.8 billion), and in France (\$16.6 billion); but less than in the USSR (\$88.7 billion). The sector of agriculture per capita in China was less than in the USSR (\$351.8), in France (\$310.2), in Japan (\$231.3), in the USA (\$195.0), and in India (\$58.3). The growth of agriculture in China was greater than in Japan (0.52%), in the United States (0.34%), and in India (0.30%); but less than in the USSR (7.0%) and in France (2.8%).

The 1980s

The value added of agriculture in China was \$94.9 billion per year in the 1980s, ranked 2nd in the world. The share in the world was 10.5%, and 27.2% in Asia.

The share of agriculture in the economy of China was 28.8% in the 1980s, ranked 38th in the world.

The Chinese agriculture per capita was \$88.5 in the 1980s, ranked 152nd in the world, and was on a par with Egypt (\$88.1), India (\$90.7). The China's agriculture per capita was less than agriculture per capita in the world (\$186.6) in 2.1 times, and was less than agriculture per capita in Asia (\$122.8) by 27.9%.

The growth of agriculture in China was 5.3% in the 1980s, ranked 20th in the world, and was on a par with the Marshall Islands (5.3%). The growth of agriculture in China (5.3%) was greater than growth of agriculture in the world (3.1%), was greater than growth of agriculture in Asia (3.8%).

Comparison with neighbors. The Chinese agriculture was greater than in India (\$70.4 billion), in Japan (\$49.7 billion), in Republic of Korea (\$13.1 billion), in Myanmar (\$3.2 billion), and in Vietnam (\$1.8 billion); but less than in the USSR (\$125.8 billion). The sector of agriculture per capita in China was greater than in Myanmar ($84.2) and in Vietnam ($29.8); but less than in the USSR ($457.2), in Japan ($410.0), in South Korea ($324.8), and in India ($90.7). The growth of agriculture in China was greater than in Vietnam (4.8%), in India (4.4%), in the USSR (2.8%), in Republic of Korea (2.6%), in Myanmar (1.6%), and in Japan (0.41%).

Comparison with leaders. The agriculture of China was greater than in India ($70.4 billion), in the USA ($68.7 billion), in Japan ($49.7 billion), and in Nigeria ($26.0 billion); but less than in the USSR ($125.8 billion). The sector of agriculture per capita in China was less than in the USSR ($457.2), in Japan ($410.0), in Nigeria ($314.5), in the USA ($286.8), and in India ($90.7). The growth of agriculture in China was greater than in India (4.4%), in the USA (3.7%), in Nigeria (3.1%), in the USSR (2.8%), and in Japan (0.41%).

The 1990s

The value added of agriculture in China was $139.0 billion per year in the 1990s, ranked 1st in the world, and was on a par with Southern Asia ($136.3 billion). The share in the world was 12.2%, and 26.5% in Asia.

The share of agriculture in the economy of China was 19.4% in the 1990s, ranked 69th in the world, and was on a par with Papua New Guinea (19.2%).

The value added of agriculture per capita in China was $112.7 in the 1990s, ranked 162nd in the world, and was on a par with Sierra Leone ($112.4), Kenya ($112.2), Myanmar ($111.0). The value added of agriculture per capita in China was less than agriculture per capita in the world ($199.8) by 43.6%, and was less than agriculture per capita in Asia ($151.6) by 25.7%.

The growth of agriculture in China was 4.3% in the 1990s, ranked 35th in the world, and was on a par with Uganda (4.3%). The growth of agriculture in China (4.3%) was greater than growth of agriculture in the world (2.2%), was greater than growth of agriculture in Asia (3.2%).

Comparison with neighbors. The sector of agriculture in China was greater than in India ($91.4 billion), in Japan ($78.9 billion), in Russia ($36.1 billion), in Republic of Korea ($24.0 billion), in Vietnam ($5.1 billion), in Myanmar ($4.9 billion), and in Kazakhstan ($4.3 billion). The sector of agriculture per capita in China was greater than in Myanmar ($111.0), in India ($95.6), and in Vietnam ($69.1); but less than in Japan ($625.5), in South Korea ($534.0), in Kazakhstan ($270.0), and in Russia ($243.9). The growth of agriculture in China was greater than in Vietnam (4.1%), in India (2.8%), in South Korea (1.4%), in Japan (-1.8%), in Russia (-5.3%), and in Kazakhstan (-7.2%); but less than in Myanmar (5.3%).

Comparison with leaders. The value of agriculture in China was greater than in the USA ($96.1 billion), in India ($91.4 billion), in Japan ($78.9 billion), in Brazil ($36.8 billion), and in Italy ($36.3 billion). The value of agriculture per capita in China was greater than in India ($95.6); but less than in Italy ($636.4), in Japan ($625.5), in the United States ($363.4), and in Brazil ($228.7). The growth of agriculture in China was greater than in Brazil (3.0%), in India (2.8%), in the United States (2.6%), in Italy (2.4%), and in Japan (-1.8%).

The 2000s

The value added of agriculture in China was $297.7 billion per year in the 2000s, ranked 1st in the world. The share in the world was 19.1%, and 37.2% in Asia.

The share of agriculture in the economy of China was 11.5% in the 2000s, ranked 84th in the world, and was on a par with Paraguay (11.6%), Cabo Verde (11.4%).

The value added of agriculture per capita in China was $224.5 in the 2000s, ranked 113th in the world, and was on a par with Gambia ($221.3), Poland ($227.7), Ivory Coast ($220.4). The value added of agriculture per capita in China was less than agriculture per capita in the world ($240.3) by 6.6%, and was greater than agriculture per capita in Asia ($202.4) by 10.9%.

The growth of agriculture in China was 4% in the 2000s, ranked 42nd in the world, and was on a par with Eswatini (4.1%). The growth of agriculture in China (4.0%) was greater than growth of agriculture in the world (3.0%), was greater than growth of agriculture in Asia (3.1%).

Comparison with neighbors. The sector of agriculture in China was greater than in India ($147.6 billion), in Japan ($57.1 billion), in Russia ($33.6 billion), in South Korea ($22.7 billion), in Vietnam ($12.1 billion), in Myanmar ($7.4 billion), and in Kazakhstan ($3.9 billion). The value added of agriculture per capita in China was greater than in Myanmar ($152.4), in Vietnam ($144.7), and in India ($129.7); but less than in Republic of Korea ($468.7), in Japan ($445.6), in Kazakhstan ($254.3), and in Russia ($232.9). The growth of agriculture in China was greater than in Vietnam (3.8%), in Russia (3.6%), in India (2.0%), in Republic of Korea (1.7%), and in

Japan (-1.3%); but less than in Myanmar (8.6%) and in Kazakhstan (4.6%).

Comparison with leaders. The China's agriculture was greater than in India ($147.6 billion), in the United States ($122.5 billion), in Japan ($57.1 billion), in Nigeria ($47.6 billion), and in Brazil ($46.2 billion). The Chinese agriculture per capita was greater than in India ($129.7); but less than in Japan ($445.6), in the United States ($416.9), in Nigeria ($346.4), and in Brazil ($250.3). The growth of agriculture in China was greater than in the United States (3.6%), in Brazil (3.4%), in India (2.0%), and in Japan (-1.3%); but less than in Nigeria (10.1%).

The 2010s

The agriculture of China was $886.2 billion per year in the 2010s, ranked 1st in the world. The share in the world was 28.0%, and 46.0% in Asia.

The share of agriculture in the economy of China was 8.4% in the 2010s, ranked 97th in the world, and was on a par with Cape Verde (8.4%), Belarus (8.4%).

The value added of agriculture per capita in China was $631.9 in the 2010s, ranked 28th in the world, and was on a par with Ireland ($630.0), Armenia ($628.8), France ($637.6). The China's agriculture per capita was greater than agriculture per capita in the world ($432.1) by 46.2%, and was greater than agriculture per capita in Asia ($436.7) by 44.7%.

The growth of agriculture in China was 3.8% in the 2010s, ranked 46th in the world, and was on a par with Congo (3.8%), Bangladesh (3.8%), Southern Asia (3.8%). The growth of agriculture in China (3.8%) was greater than growth of agriculture in the world (2.9%), was greater than growth of agriculture in Asia (3.3%).

Comparison with neighbors. The China's agriculture was 2.4 times higher than in India ($363.4 billion), 14.7 times higher than in Russia ($60.3 billion), 14.9 times higher than in Japan ($59.6 billion), 28.2 times higher than in Vietnam ($31.5 billion), 31.2 times higher than in South Korea ($28.4 billion), 50.7 times higher than in Myanmar ($17.5 billion), and 105.6 times higher than in Kazakhstan ($8.4 billion). The sector of agriculture per capita in China was 12.7% higher than in Republic of Korea ($560.9), 31.2% higher than in Kazakhstan ($481.8), 35.6% higher than in Japan ($466.2), 51.7% higher than in Russia ($416.5), 85.1% higher than in Vietnam ($341.3), 89.3% higher than in Myanmar ($333.8), and 2.3 times higher than in India ($279.1). The growth of agriculture in China was greater than in Vietnam (2.6%), in Kazakhstan (2.0%), in Myanmar (1.3%), in Russia (1.2%), in Republic of Korea (0.25%), and in Japan (-1.9%); but less than in India (4.1%).

Comparison with leaders. The value added of agriculture in China was 2.4 times higher than in India ($363.4 billion), 4.9 times higher than in the USA ($180.3 billion), 7.1 times higher than in Indonesia ($124.1 billion), 9.3 times higher than in Nigeria ($95.8 billion), and 9.3 times higher than in Brazil ($95.1 billion). The agriculture per capita in China was 12.0% higher than in the USA ($564.3), 18.2% higher than in Nigeria ($534.6), 30.7% higher than in Indonesia ($483.6), 35.3% higher than in Brazil ($467.2), and 2.3 times higher than in India ($279.1). The growth of agriculture in China was greater than in Nigeria (3.6%), in Brazil (3.4%), and in the USA (2.0%); but less than in India (4.1%) and in Indonesia (3.9%).

Chapter V. Industry

Mining, Manufacturing, Utilities (ISIC C-E)

The sector of industry in China enlarged from $64.3 billion per year in the 1970s to $3.7 trillion per year in the 2010s, that is by $3.6 trillion or 57.3 times. The change occurred at -$301.3 billion due to a 1.1-fold decrease in prices, as also at $3.9 trillion due to a 40.4-fold increase in productivity, as well as at $34.3 billion due to the increase in population. The average annual growth in industry is 10.2%. The minimum value of industry was in 1970 at $34.0 billion. The maximum value of industry was in 2019 at $4.6 trillion.

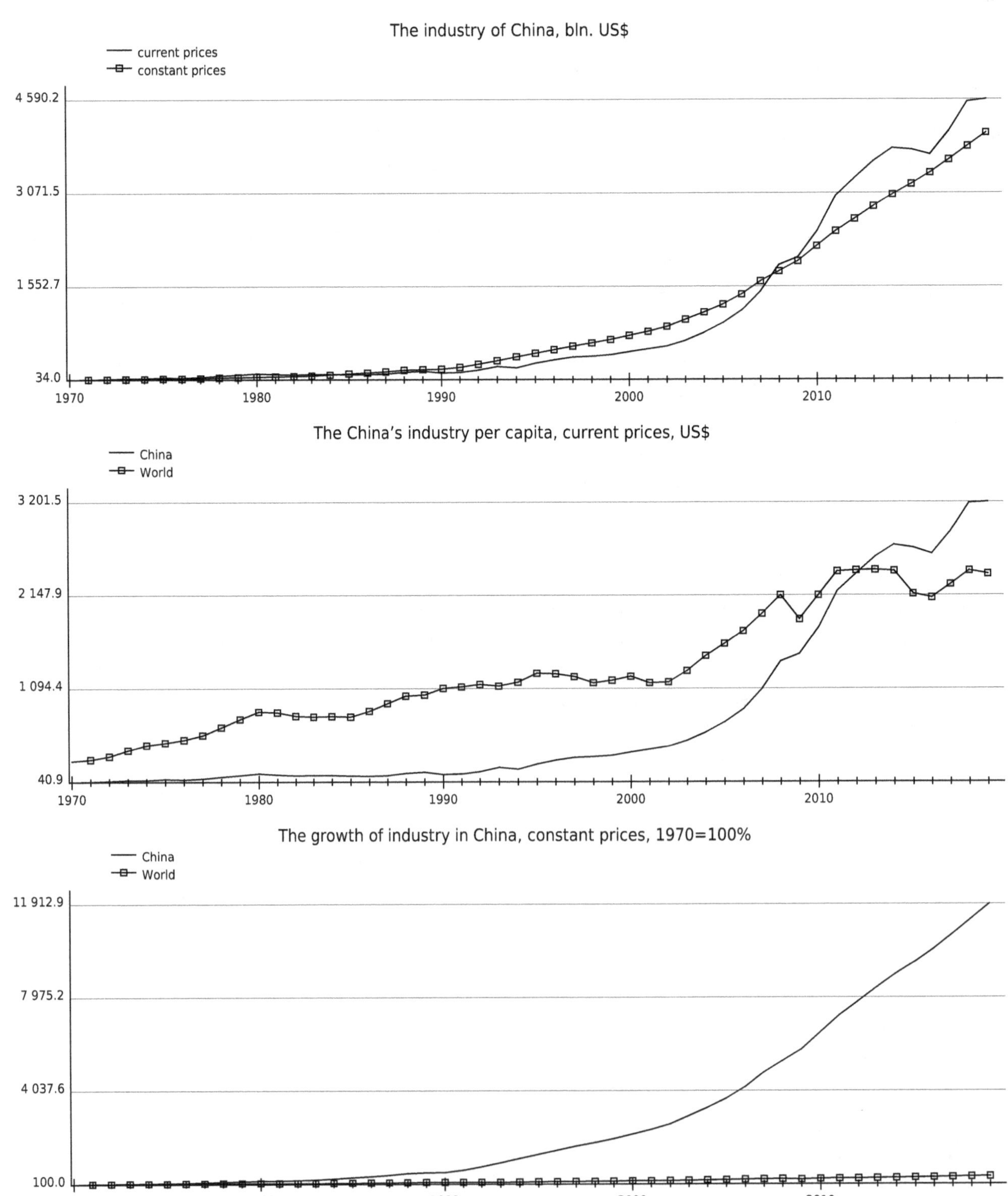

The industry of China, bln. US$

The China's industry per capita, current prices, US$

The growth of industry in China, constant prices, 1970=100%

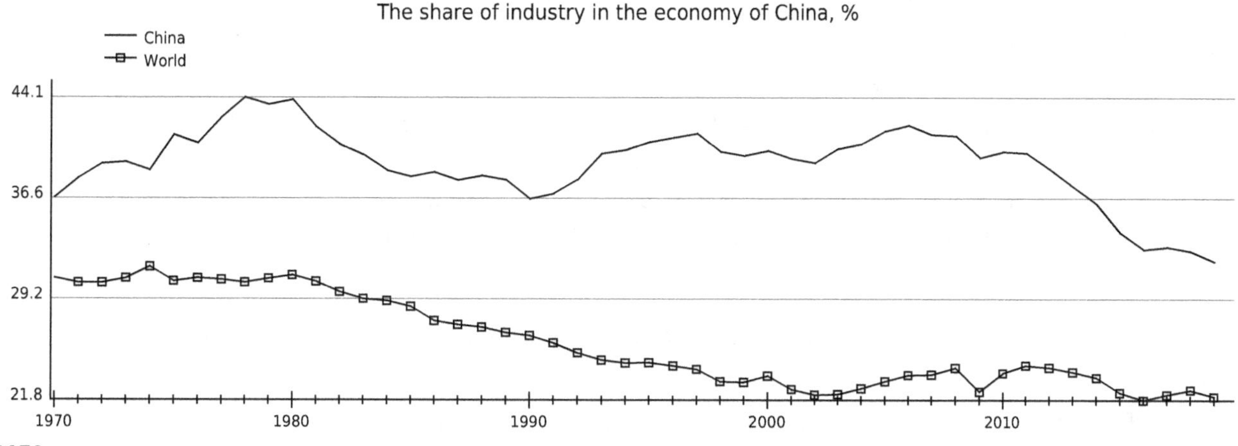

The 1970s

The industry of China was $64.3 billion per year in the 1970s, ranked 7th in the world. The share in the world was 3.3%, and 15.9% in Asia.

The share of industry in the economy of China was 41.1% in the 1970s, ranked 15th in the world, and was on a par with Poland (40.9%), Namibia (40.9%), Trinidad and Tobago (41.4%).

The sector of industry per capita in China was $70.3 in the 1970s, ranked 127th in the world, and was on a par with Egypt ($70.0), Djibouti ($69.8), El Salvador ($69.6). The value added of industry per capita in China was less than industry per capita in the world ($480.5) in 6.8 times, and was less than industry per capita in Asia ($173.9) in 2.5 times.

The growth of industry in China was 8.9% in the 1970s, ranked 26th in the world, and was on a par with the Solomon Islands (9.0%). The growth of industry in China (8.9%) was greater than growth of industry in the world (4.0%), was greater than growth of industry in Asia (5.7%).

Comparison with neighbors. The China's industry was greater than in India ($18.4 billion), in Republic of Korea ($6.4 billion), in Vietnam ($877.9 million), and in Myanmar ($386.9 million); but less than in the USSR ($248.8 billion) and in Japan ($185.6 billion). The sector of industry per capita in China was greater than in India ($29.9), in Vietnam ($18.3), and in Myanmar ($12.8); but less than in Japan ($1 666.5), in the USSR ($986.6), and in South Korea ($181.7). The growth of industry in China was greater than in the USSR (5.2%), in Vietnam (4.7%), in India (4.6%), in Japan (4.5%), and in Myanmar (3.3%); but less than in Republic of Korea (15.2%).

Comparison with leaders. The industry of China was less than in the USA ($450.4 billion), in the USSR ($248.8 billion), in Japan ($185.6 billion), in Germany ($158.4 billion), and in the United Kingdom ($72.6 billion). The industry per capita in China was less than in the United States ($2.1 thousand), in Germany ($2.0 thousand), in Japan ($1 666.5), in the UK ($1 295.1), and in the USSR ($986.6). The growth of industry in China was greater than in the USSR (5.2%), in Japan (4.5%), in the United States (2.4%), in Germany (2.1%), and in the United Kingdom (1.9%).

The 1980s

The value of industry in China was $130.2 billion per year in the 1980s, ranked 8th in the world. The share in the world was 3.1%, and 12.1% in Asia.

The share of industry in the economy of China was 39.5% in the 1980s, ranked 18th in the world.

The industry per capita in China was $121.4 in the 1980s, ranked 129th in the world. The value added of industry per capita in China was less than industry per capita in the world ($861.8) in 7.1 times, and was less than industry per capita in Asia ($380.7) in 3.1 times.

The growth of industry in China was 10.4% in the 1980s, ranked 10th in the world. The growth of industry in China (10.4%) was greater than growth of industry in the world (2.3%), was greater than growth of industry in Asia (3.5%).

Comparison with neighbors. The value of industry in China was greater than in India ($51.0 billion), in South Korea ($34.9 billion), in Vietnam ($847.1 million), and in Myanmar ($596.8 million); but less than in Japan ($566.4 billion) and in the USSR ($305.7 billion). The sector of industry per capita in China was greater than in India ($65.7), in Myanmar ($15.9), and in Vietnam ($14.0); but less than in Japan ($4.7 thousand), in the USSR ($1 110.8), and in Republic of Korea ($863.0). The growth of industry in China was greater than in South Korea (10.2%), in India (7.4%), in the USSR (5.3%), in Vietnam (4.8%), in Japan (4.2%), and in Myanmar (1.5%).

Comparison with leaders. The value added of industry in China was less than in the United States ($1.0 trillion), in Japan ($566.4 billion), in the USSR ($305.7 billion), in Germany ($297.5 billion), and in the United Kingdom ($171.2 billion). The value of industry per capita in China was less than in Japan ($4.7 thousand), in the United States ($4.2 thousand), in Germany ($3.8 thousand), in the UK ($3.0 thousand), and in the USSR ($1 110.8). The growth of industry in China was greater than in the USSR (5.3%), in Japan (4.2%), in the United States (1.9%), in the United Kingdom (1.4%), and in Germany (1.2%).

The 1990s

The sector of industry in China was $285.9 billion per year in the 1990s, ranked 4th in the world. The share in the world was 4.3%, and 12.9% in Asia.

The share of industry in the economy of China was 39.9% in the 1990s, ranked 15th in the world.

The industry per capita in China was $231.9 in the 1990s, ranked 133rd in the world. The Chinese industry per capita was less than industry per capita in the world ($1 175.6) in 5.1 times, and was less than industry per capita in Asia ($639.7) in 2.8 times.

The growth of industry in China was 13.1% in the 1990s, ranked 7th in the world, and was on a par with Laos (13.1%). The growth of industry in China (13.1%) was greater than growth of industry in the world (2.5%), was greater than growth of industry in Asia (5.5%).

Comparison with neighbors. The Chinese industry was greater than in Russia ($138.6 billion), in Republic of Korea ($123.3 billion), in India ($78.9 billion), in Kazakhstan ($5.2 billion), in Vietnam ($4.5 billion), and in Myanmar ($576.3 million); but less than in Japan ($1.2 trillion). The industry per capita in China was greater than in India ($82.6), in Vietnam ($60.2), and in Myanmar ($13.2); but less than in Japan ($9.4 thousand), in South Korea ($2.7 thousand), in Russia ($937.0), and in Kazakhstan ($329.2). The growth of industry in China was greater than in Myanmar (9.8%), in South Korea (8.7%), in India (5.8%), in Japan (1.3%), in Kazakhstan (-2.7%), and in Russia (-6.8%); but less than in Vietnam (13.4%).

Comparison with leaders. The China's industry was greater than in the UK ($268.6 billion) and in Italy ($259.5 billion); but less than in the United States ($1.5 trillion), in Japan ($1.2 trillion), and in Germany ($534.0 billion). The value of industry per capita in China was less than in Japan ($9.4 thousand), in Germany ($6.6 thousand), in the United States ($5.7 thousand), in the United Kingdom ($4.6 thousand), and in Italy ($4.6 thousand). The growth of industry in China was greater than in the United States (2.8%), in Japan (1.3%), in the UK (1.2%), in Italy (1.0%), and in Germany (0.33%).

The 2000s

The sector of industry in China was $1.1 trillion per year in the 2000s, ranked 3rd in the world. The share in the world was 10.3%, and 28.0% in Asia.

The share of industry in the economy of China was 40.7% in the 2000s, ranked 20th in the world.

The value of industry per capita in China was $795.3 in the 2000s, ranked 103rd in the world. The value of industry per capita in China was less than industry per capita in the world ($1 573.8) by 49.5%, and was less than industry per capita in Asia ($951.8) by 16.4%.

The growth of industry in China was 11.1% in the 2000s, ranked 11th in the world. The growth of industry in China (11.1%) was greater than growth of industry in the world (2.9%), was greater than growth of industry in Asia (5.7%).

Comparison with neighbors. The sector of industry in China was greater than in South Korea ($233.7 billion), in Russia ($207.1 billion), in India ($179.9 billion), in Vietnam ($19.0 billion), in Kazakhstan ($19.0 billion), and in Myanmar ($2.6 billion); but less than in Japan ($1.1 trillion). The China's industry per capita was greater than in Vietnam ($228.2), in India ($158.0), and in Myanmar ($52.8); but less than in Japan ($8.8 thousand), in Republic of Korea ($4.8 thousand), in Russia ($1 435.1), and in Kazakhstan ($1 238.4). The growth of industry in China was greater than in Kazakhstan (8.3%), in Vietnam (7.4%), in India (7.0%), in Republic of Korea (6.4%), in Russia (3.5%), and in Japan (0.15%); but less than in Myanmar (19.5%).

Comparison with leaders. The value added of industry in China was greater than in Germany ($629.4 billion), in the UK ($345.1 billion), and in Italy ($320.8 billion); but less than in the USA ($2.1 trillion) and in Japan ($1.1 trillion). The industry per capita in China was less than in Japan ($8.8 thousand), in Germany ($7.7 thousand), in the United States ($7.1 thousand), in the United Kingdom ($5.7 thousand), and in Italy ($5.5 thousand). The growth of industry in China was greater than in the United States (1.5%), in

Germany (0.19%), in Japan (0.15%), in the United Kingdom (-1.1%), and in Italy (-1.4%).

The 2010s

The Chinese industry was $3.7 trillion per year in the 2010s, ranked 1st in the world. The share in the world was 21.6%, and 45.2% in Asia.

The share of industry in the economy of China was 35.1% in the 2010s, ranked 23rd in the world, and was on a par with Malaysia (35.0%).

The value of industry per capita in China was $2 626.2 in the 2010s, ranked 59th in the world, and was on a par with Azerbaijan ($2.6 thousand). The sector of industry per capita in China was greater than industry per capita in the world ($2 320.9) by 13.2%, and was greater than industry per capita in Asia ($1 847.0) by 42.2%.

The growth of industry in China was 7.5% in the 2010s, ranked 20th in the world. The growth of industry in China (7.5%) was greater than growth of industry in the world (3.5%), was greater than growth of industry in Asia (5.6%).

Comparison with neighbors. The sector of industry in China was 3.1 times higher than in Japan ($1.2 trillion), 8.3 times higher than in India ($443.4 billion), 8.7 times higher than in Republic of Korea ($422.5 billion), 9.0 times higher than in Russia ($410.4 billion), 70.0 times higher than in Vietnam ($52.6 billion), 70.3 times higher than in Kazakhstan ($52.4 billion), and 198.9 times higher than in Myanmar ($18.5 billion). The sector of industry per capita in China was 4.6 times higher than in Vietnam ($570.7), 7.4 times higher than in Myanmar ($353.4), and 7.7 times higher than in India ($340.6); but 3.5 times lower than in Japan ($9.3 thousand), 3.2 times lower than in South Korea ($8.4 thousand), 12.7% lower than in Kazakhstan ($3.0 thousand), and 7.4% lower than in Russia ($2.8 thousand). The growth of industry in China was greater than in India (6.5%), in Vietnam (5.6%), in South Korea (3.6%), in Kazakhstan (3.2%), in Japan (2.6%), and in Russia (1.7%); but less than in Myanmar (9.6%).

Comparison with leaders. The sector of industry in China was 34.3% higher than in the United States ($2.7 trillion), 3.1 times higher than in Japan ($1.2 trillion), 4.4 times higher than in Germany ($840.0 billion), 8.3 times higher than in India ($443.4 billion), and 8.7 times higher than in South Korea ($422.5 billion). The industry per capita in China was 7.7 times higher than in India ($340.6); but 3.9 times lower than in Germany ($10.3 thousand), 3.5 times lower than in Japan ($9.3 thousand), 3.3 times lower than in the USA ($8.6 thousand), and 3.2 times lower than in Republic of Korea ($8.4 thousand). The growth of industry in China was greater than in India (6.5%), in Republic of Korea (3.6%), in Germany (3.2%), in Japan (2.6%), and in the USA (2.2%).

Chapter VI. Construction

(ISIC F)

The sector of construction in China grew from $6.1 billion per year in the 1970s to $731.1 billion per year in the 2010s, that is by $725.0 billion or 120.3 times. The change occurred at $462.3 billion due to a 2.7-fold increase in prices, as also at $259.4 billion due to a 28.8-fold increase in productivity, as well as at $3.2 billion due to the rise in population. The average annual growth in construction is 9.2%. The minimum value of construction was in 1970 at $3.4 billion. The maximum value of construction was in 2019 at $1.0 trillion.

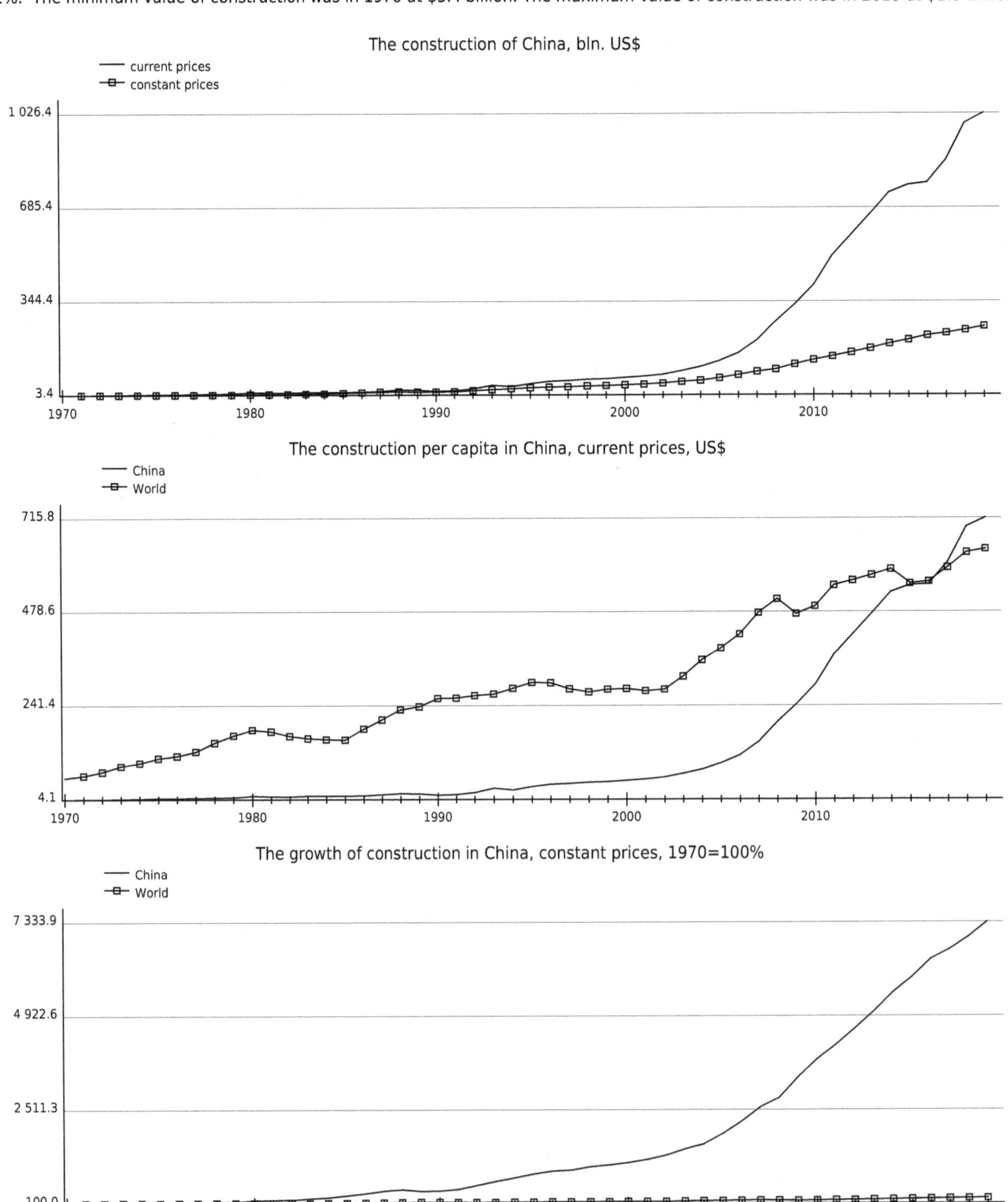

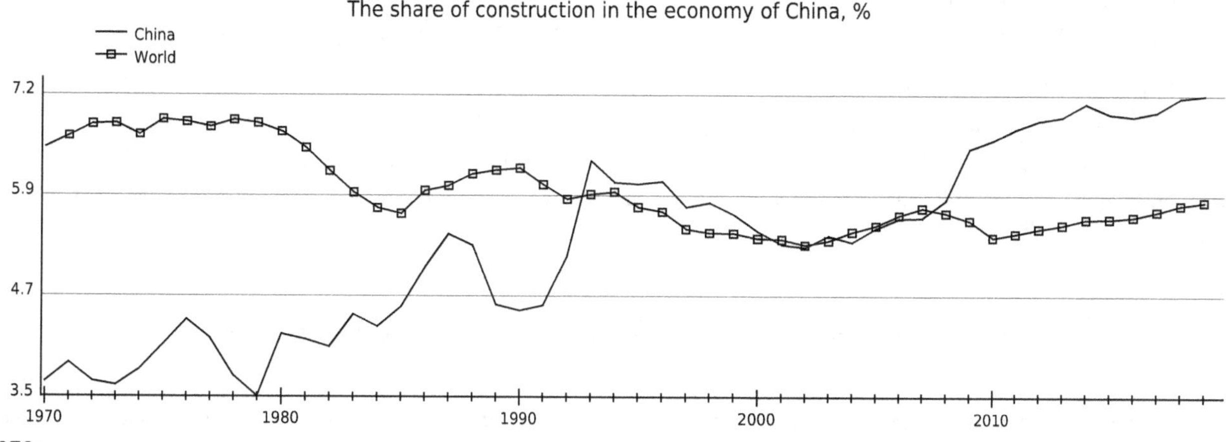

The share of construction in the economy of China, %

The 1970s

The Chinese construction was $6.1 billion per year in the 1970s, ranked 15th in the world, and was on a par with Brazil ($6.1 billion). The share in the world was 1.4%, and 7.6% in Asia.

The share of construction in the economy of China was 3.9% in the 1970s, ranked 143rd in the world, and was on a par with Egypt (3.9%).

The construction per capita in China was $6.7 in the 1970s, ranked 167th in the world, and was on a par with Benin ($6.6). The sector of construction per capita in China was less than construction per capita in the world ($106.1) in 16.0 times, and was less than construction per capita in Asia ($34.4) in 5.2 times.

The growth of construction in China was 4.4% in the 1970s, ranked 96th in the world. The growth of construction in China (4.4%) was greater than growth of construction in the world (2.1%), was less than growth of construction in Asia (5.1%).

Comparison with neighbors. The construction of China was greater than in India ($4.3 billion), in South Korea ($1.5 billion), in Vietnam ($145.1 million), and in Myanmar ($44.4 million); but less than in the USSR ($52.5 billion) and in Japan ($43.5 billion). The construction per capita in China was greater than in Vietnam ($3.0) and in Myanmar ($1.5); but less than in Japan ($390.8), in the USSR ($208.1), in South Korea ($41.8), and in India ($7.0). The growth of construction in China was greater than in Japan (3.4%) and in India (2.0%); but less than in Republic of Korea (11.3%), in Myanmar (6.5%), in the USSR (6.5%), and in Vietnam (4.7%).

Comparison with leaders. The construction of China was less than in the USA ($81.1 billion), in the USSR ($52.5 billion), in Japan ($43.5 billion), in Germany ($33.8 billion), and in France ($22.4 billion). The construction per capita in China was less than in Germany ($428.6), in France ($417.3), in Japan ($390.8), in the USA ($371.5), and in the USSR ($208.1). The growth of construction in China was greater than in Japan (3.4%), in France (2.0%), in Germany (0.66%), and in the USA (0.31%); but less than in the USSR (6.5%).

The 1980s

The Chinese construction was $15.5 billion per year in the 1980s, ranked 12th in the world. The share in the world was 1.7%, and 6.6% in Asia.

The share of construction in the economy of China was 4.7% in the 1980s, ranked 123rd in the world, and was on a par with Rwanda (4.7%), Niger (4.7%).

The construction per capita in China was $14.4 in the 1980s, ranked 158th in the world. The sector of construction per capita in China was less than construction per capita in the world ($186.2) in 12.9 times, and was less than construction per capita in Asia ($83.3) in 5.8 times.

The growth of construction in China was 11.2% in the 1980s, ranked 3rd in the world, and was on a par with Antigua and Barbuda (11.2%). The growth of construction in China (11.2%) was greater than growth of construction in the world (1.7%), was greater than growth of construction in Asia (2.7%).

Comparison with neighbors. The construction of China was greater than in India ($11.7 billion), in South Korea ($7.3 billion), in Vietnam ($141.5 million), and in Myanmar ($87.1 million); but less than in Japan ($138.7 billion) and in the USSR ($72.1 billion). The value added of construction per capita in China was greater than in Vietnam ($2.3) and in Myanmar ($2.3); but less than in Japan ($1

143.9), in the USSR ($262.0), in South Korea ($180.7), and in India ($15.1). The growth of construction in China was greater than in Republic of Korea (6.9%), in the USSR (6.2%), in Myanmar (5.2%), in India (5.0%), in Vietnam (4.6%), and in Japan (2.1%).

Comparison with leaders. The construction of China was less than in the United States ($180.6 billion), in Japan ($138.7 billion), in the USSR ($72.1 billion), in Germany ($57.8 billion), and in France ($42.5 billion). The value of construction per capita in China was less than in Japan ($1 143.9), in the USA ($754.4), in France ($751.9), in Germany ($740.2), and in the USSR ($262.0). The growth of construction in China was greater than in the USSR (6.2%), in Japan (2.1%), in the USA (1.1%), in France (0.67%), and in Germany (-0.52%).

The 1990s

The construction of China was $41.3 billion per year in the 1990s, ranked 8th in the world. The share in the world was 2.6%, and 7.5% in Asia.

The share of construction in the economy of China was 5.8% in the 1990s, ranked 100th in the world, and was on a par with Slovenia (5.8%), Aruba (5.7%), the World (5.8%).

The sector of construction per capita in China was $33.5 in the 1990s, ranked 160th in the world, and was on a par with Angola ($33.7). The value of construction per capita in China was less than construction per capita in the world ($278.6) in 8.3 times, and was less than construction per capita in Asia ($158.8) in 4.7 times.

The growth of construction in China was 9.9% in the 1990s, ranked 22nd in the world, and was on a par with El Salvador (9.8%), Vietnam (9.9%). The growth of construction in China (9.9%) was greater than growth of construction in the world (0.71%), was greater than growth of construction in Asia (2.3%).

Comparison with neighbors. The construction of China was greater than in South Korea ($36.3 billion), in Russia ($34.1 billion), in India ($18.9 billion), in Kazakhstan ($1.7 billion), in Vietnam ($1.1 billion), and in Myanmar ($145.3 million); but less than in Japan ($343.2 billion). The construction per capita in China was greater than in India ($19.8), in Vietnam ($15.1), and in Myanmar ($3.3); but less than in Japan ($2.7 thousand), in South Korea ($806.8), in Russia ($230.4), and in Kazakhstan ($105.3). The growth of construction in China was greater than in India (5.6%), in Republic of Korea (3.8%), in Japan (-1.0%), in Russia (-12.1%), and in Kazakhstan (-15.2%); but less than in Myanmar (14.4%) and in Vietnam (9.9%).

Comparison with leaders. The Chinese construction was less than in Japan ($343.2 billion), in the United States ($299.1 billion), in Germany ($125.2 billion), in the United Kingdom ($69.8 billion), and in France ($68.8 billion). The value added of construction per capita in China was less than in Japan ($2.7 thousand), in Germany ($1 552.3), in the United Kingdom ($1 205.1), in France ($1 158.8), and in the USA ($1 131.2). The growth of construction in China was greater than in the USA (1.8%), in Germany (-0.047%), in the UK (-0.34%), in France (-0.65%), and in Japan (-1.0%).

The 2000s

The construction of China was $150.1 billion per year in the 2000s, ranked 3rd in the world. The share in the world was 6.1%, and 20.9% in Asia.

The share of construction in the economy of China was 5.8% in the 2000s, ranked 104th in the world, and was on a par with Japan (5.8%), Papua New Guinea (5.8%), Bermuda (5.8%).

The sector of construction per capita in China was $113.1 in the 2000s, ranked 129th in the world, and was on a par with Northern Africa ($111.0). The value added of construction per capita in China was less than construction per capita in the world ($381.3) in 3.4 times, and was less than construction per capita in Asia ($181.9) by 37.8%.

The growth of construction in China was 11.9% in the 2000s, ranked 28th in the world. The growth of construction in China (11.9%) was greater than growth of construction in the world (1.5%), was greater than growth of construction in Asia (4.4%).

Comparison with neighbors. The value added of construction in China was greater than in India ($66.2 billion), in South Korea ($47.5 billion), in Russia ($40.5 billion), in Kazakhstan ($5.0 billion), in Vietnam ($3.6 billion), and in Myanmar ($604.6 million); but less than in Japan ($270.5 billion). The sector of construction per capita in China was greater than in India ($58.2), in Vietnam ($42.6), and in Myanmar ($12.4); but less than in Japan ($2.1 thousand), in Republic of Korea ($979.3), in Kazakhstan ($327.8), and in Russia ($280.3). The growth of construction in China was greater than in Vietnam (9.5%), in India (9.3%), in Russia (8.1%), in South Korea (1.5%), and in Japan (-3.9%); but less than in Myanmar (19.9%) and in Kazakhstan (17.2%).

Comparison with leaders. The construction of China was greater than in the UK ($132.1 billion), in Spain ($111.8 billion), and in France ($106.0 billion); but less than in the USA ($583.0 billion) and in Japan ($270.5 billion). The value added of construction per capita in China was less than in Spain ($2.6 thousand), in the UK ($2.2 thousand), in Japan ($2.1 thousand), in the United States ($1 983.7), and in France ($1 688.4). The growth of construction in China was greater than in Spain (1.7%), in France (1.3%), in the United Kingdom (0.17%), in the USA (-2.6%), and in Japan (-3.9%).

The 2010s

The Chinese construction was $731.1 billion per year in the 2010s, ranked 1st in the world. The share in the world was 17.4%, and 42.2% in Asia.

The share of construction in the economy of China was 7.0% in the 2010s, ranked 73rd in the world, and was on a par with Eastern Europe (7.0%), Central Asia (7.0%).

The sector of construction per capita in China was $521.3 in the 2010s, ranked 88th in the world, and was on a par with Suriname ($521.6), Hungary ($524.2), Brazil ($527.4). The construction per capita in China was less than construction per capita in the world ($572.1) by 8.9%, and was greater than construction per capita in Asia ($392.9) by 32.7%.

The growth of construction in China was 8.2% in the 2010s, ranked 29th in the world, and was on a par with Bhutan (8.1%), Turkmenistan (8.1%), Nauru (8.2%). The growth of construction in China (8.2%) was greater than growth of construction in the world (2.9%), was greater than growth of construction in Asia (5.6%).

Comparison with neighbors. The sector of construction in China was 2.6 times higher than in Japan ($278.7 billion), 4.3 times higher than in India ($168.1 billion), 6.4 times higher than in Russia ($114.9 billion), 10.2 times higher than in South Korea ($71.9 billion), 65.5 times higher than in Kazakhstan ($11.2 billion), 68.9 times higher than in Vietnam ($10.6 billion), and 200.9 times higher than in Myanmar ($3.6 billion). The value added of construction per capita in China was 4.0 times higher than in India ($129.1), 4.5 times higher than in Vietnam ($115.2), and 7.5 times higher than in Myanmar ($69.4); but 4.2 times lower than in Japan ($2.2 thousand), 2.7 times lower than in Republic of Korea ($1 422.3), 34.3% lower than in Russia ($793.7), and 18.7% lower than in Kazakhstan ($640.9). The growth of construction in China was greater than in Vietnam (6.8%), in India (5.2%), in Kazakhstan (4.8%), in Russia (1.8%), in Japan (1.7%), and in South Korea (1.2%); but less than in Myanmar (10.2%).

Comparison with leaders. The China's construction was 7.4% higher than in the United States ($680.8 billion), 2.6 times higher than in Japan ($278.7 billion), 4.3 times higher than in India ($168.1 billion), 4.8 times higher than in Germany ($153.2 billion), and 4.8 times higher than in the United Kingdom ($152.6 billion). The China's construction per capita was 4.0 times higher than in India ($129.1); but 4.5 times lower than in the United Kingdom ($2.3 thousand), 4.2 times lower than in Japan ($2.2 thousand), 4.1 times lower than in the United States ($2.1 thousand), and 3.6 times lower than in Germany ($1 871.9). The growth of construction in China was greater than in India (5.2%), in the UK (2.9%), in Germany (1.8%), in Japan (1.7%), and in the USA (1.4%).

Chapter VII. Transportation

Transport, storage and communication (ISIC I)

The transportation of China increased from $7.5 billion per year in the 1970s to $464.2 billion per year in the 2010s, that is by $456.7 billion or 61.9 times. The change occurred at $215.3 billion due to a 1.9-fold increase in prices, as also at $237.5 billion due to a 21.6-fold increase in productivity, as well as at $4.0 billion due to the growing in population. The average annual growth in transportation is 8.8%. The minimum value of transportation was in 1970 at $4.1 billion. The maximum value of transportation was in 2019 at $619.6 billion.

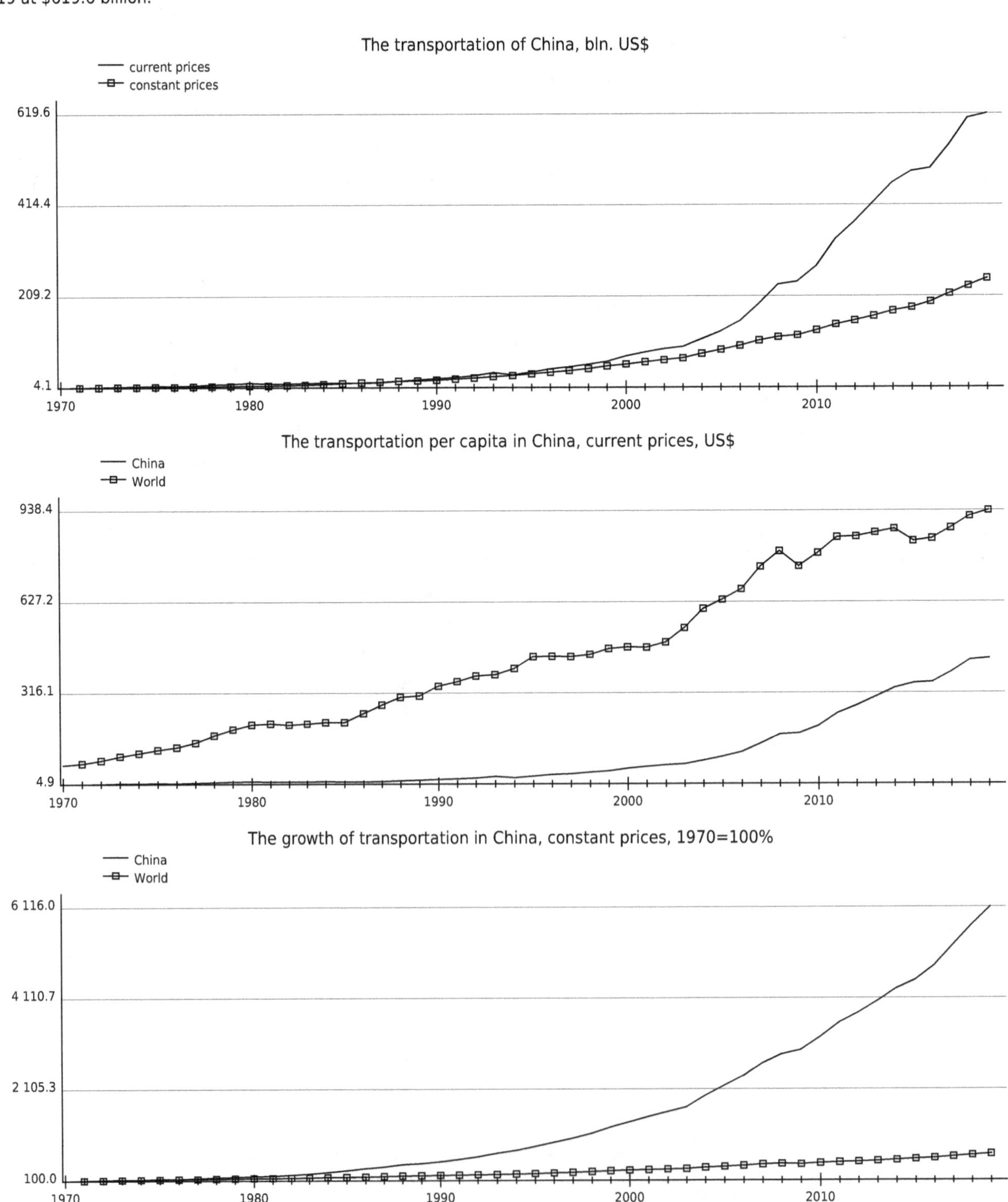

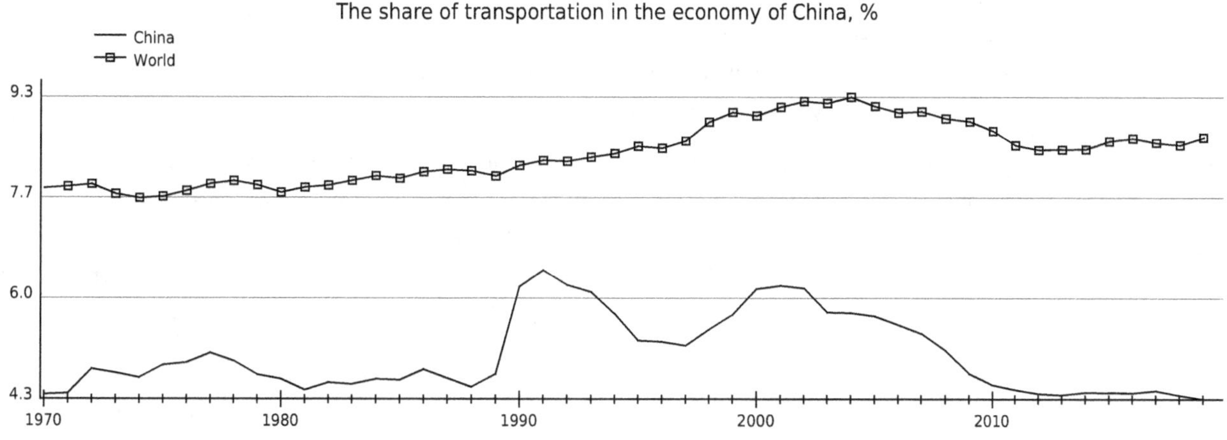

The 1970s

The transportation of China was $7.5 billion per year in the 1970s, ranked 11th in the world, and was on a par with Australia ($7.4 billion), Spain ($7.6 billion). The share in the world was 1.5%, and 9.4% in Asia.

The share of transportation in the economy of China was 4.8% in the 1970s, ranked 136th in the world, and was on a par with the Comoros (4.8%), Romania (4.8%), Guyana (4.8%).

The Chinese transportation per capita was $8.2 in the 1970s, ranked 165th in the world. The sector of transportation per capita in China was less than transportation per capita in the world ($122.3) in 14.9 times, and was less than transportation per capita in Asia ($34.3) in 4.2 times.

The growth of transportation in China was 6.8% in the 1970s, ranked 68th in the world, and was on a par with Tonga (6.8%), Africa (6.8%). The growth of transportation in China (6.8%) was greater than growth of transportation in the world (4.6%), was greater than growth of transportation in Asia (4.1%).

Comparison with neighbors. The value added of transportation in China was greater than in India ($3.5 billion), in South Korea ($1.8 billion), in Myanmar ($176.0 million), and in Vietnam ($111.6 million); but less than in Japan ($46.4 billion) and in the USSR ($28.8 billion). The value added of transportation per capita in China was greater than in Myanmar ($5.8), in India ($5.7), and in Vietnam ($2.3); but less than in Japan ($416.6), in the USSR ($114.0), and in South Korea ($50.2). The growth of transportation in China was greater than in India (6.1%), in Vietnam (4.7%), in Myanmar (2.7%), and in Japan (1.7%); but less than in Republic of Korea (12.2%) and in the USSR (8.1%).

Comparison with leaders. The transportation of China was less than in the United States ($168.6 billion), in Japan ($46.4 billion), in Germany ($29.6 billion), in the USSR ($28.8 billion), and in France ($24.0 billion). The value added of transportation per capita in China was less than in the USA ($772.4), in France ($447.4), in Japan ($416.6), in Germany ($376.1), and in the USSR ($114.0). The growth of transportation in China was greater than in the United States (4.2%), in France (4.1%), in Germany (3.0%), and in Japan (1.7%); but less than in the USSR (8.1%).

The 1980s

The Chinese transportation was $15.3 billion per year in the 1980s, ranked 12th in the world, and was on a par with Mexico ($15.3 billion). The share in the world was 1.3%, and 6.2% in Asia.

The share of transportation in the economy of China was 4.6% in the 1980s, ranked 149th in the world.

The sector of transportation per capita in China was $14.3 in the 1980s, ranked 164th in the world. The value added of transportation per capita in China was less than transportation per capita in the world ($242.0) in 17.0 times, and was less than transportation per capita in Asia ($86.8) in 6.1 times.

The growth of transportation in China was 10.1% in the 1980s, ranked 10th in the world, and was on a par with the Cayman Islands (10.0%), the British Virgin Islands (10.0%), Gambia (10.2%). The growth of transportation in China (10.1%) was greater than growth of transportation in the world (3.4%), was greater than growth of transportation in Asia (5.2%).

Comparison with neighbors. The sector of transportation in China was greater than in India ($10.6 billion), in Republic of Korea ($8.6

billion), in Myanmar ($276.3 million), and in Vietnam ($107.1 million); but less than in Japan ($147.7 billion) and in the USSR ($39.1 billion). The Chinese transportation per capita was greater than in India ($13.7), in Myanmar ($7.4), and in Vietnam ($1.8); but less than in Japan ($1 217.8), in Republic of Korea ($213.3), and in the USSR ($142.2). The growth of transportation in China was greater than in Republic of Korea (8.0%), in India (7.1%), in Japan (4.7%), in Vietnam (4.4%), in Myanmar (4.0%), and in the USSR (1.8%).

Comparison with leaders. The sector of transportation in China was less than in the USA ($394.9 billion), in Japan ($147.7 billion), in Germany ($56.6 billion), in France ($56.2 billion), and in the UK ($53.0 billion). The China's transportation per capita was less than in the USA ($1 649.2), in Japan ($1 217.8), in France ($993.7), in the UK ($938.7), and in Germany ($725.5). The growth of transportation in China was greater than in France (5.4%), in Japan (4.7%), in the USA (3.6%), in the UK (3.0%), and in Germany (1.8%).

The 1990s

The transportation of China was $40.5 billion per year in the 1990s, ranked 9th in the world, and was on a par with Southern Asia ($40.3 billion). The share in the world was 1.7%, and 6.6% in Asia.

The share of transportation in the economy of China was 5.7% in the 1990s, ranked 165th in the world, and was on a par with Algeria (5.7%).

The sector of transportation per capita in China was $32.9 in the 1990s, ranked 167th in the world, and was on a par with Armenia ($32.8), Mauritania ($32.3). The value of transportation per capita in China was less than transportation per capita in the world ($409.5) in 12.5 times, and was less than transportation per capita in Asia ($177.2) in 5.4 times.

The growth of transportation in China was 10.4% in the 1990s, ranked 14th in the world, and was on a par with Bhutan (10.3%). The growth of transportation in China (10.4%) was greater than growth of transportation in the world (4.0%), was greater than growth of transportation in Asia (5.4%).

Comparison with neighbors. The Chinese transportation was greater than in Russia ($38.4 billion), in Republic of Korea ($31.6 billion), in India ($21.1 billion), in Kazakhstan ($2.4 billion), in Vietnam ($738.7 million), and in Myanmar ($326.3 million); but less than in Japan ($373.9 billion). The transportation per capita in China was greater than in India ($22.1), in Vietnam ($10.0), and in Myanmar ($7.5); but less than in Japan ($3.0 thousand), in South Korea ($702.9), in Russia ($259.8), and in Kazakhstan ($151.2). The growth of transportation in China was greater than in South Korea (9.9%), in India (7.7%), in Vietnam (6.7%), in Japan (3.0%), in Russia (-7.1%), and in Kazakhstan (-8.7%); but less than in Myanmar (10.7%).

Comparison with leaders. The value added of transportation in China was less than in the United States ($702.6 billion), in Japan ($373.9 billion), in Germany ($144.3 billion), in France ($118.7 billion), and in the UK ($117.6 billion). The value of transportation per capita in China was less than in Japan ($3.0 thousand), in the United States ($2.7 thousand), in the United Kingdom ($2.0 thousand), in France ($1 999.2), and in Germany ($1 789.0). The growth of transportation in China was greater than in the United States (5.0%), in France (4.8%), in the UK (4.7%), in Germany (3.9%), and in Japan (3.0%).

The 2000s

The value of transportation in China was $140.8 billion per year in the 2000s, ranked 7th in the world. The share in the world was 3.5%, and 13.5% in Asia.

The share of transportation in the economy of China was 5.4% in the 2000s, ranked 181st in the world, and was on a par with Gabon (5.4%), Malawi (5.4%).

The transportation per capita in China was $106.2 in the 2000s, ranked 150th in the world, and was on a par with Indonesia ($103.9). The value of transportation per capita in China was less than transportation per capita in the world ($621.1) in 5.8 times, and was less than transportation per capita in Asia ($264.8) in 2.5 times.

The growth of transportation in China was 8.8% in the 2000s, ranked 44th in the world, and was on a par with Panama (8.8%), Laos (8.8%), Iran (8.8%). The growth of transportation in China (8.8%) was greater than growth of transportation in the world (3.9%), was greater than growth of transportation in Asia (5.4%).

Comparison with neighbors. The value added of transportation in China was greater than in South Korea ($71.3 billion), in Russia ($65.2 billion), in India ($55.5 billion), in Kazakhstan ($7.2 billion), in Vietnam ($2.5 billion), and in Myanmar ($1.9 billion); but less than in Japan ($468.5 billion). The Chinese transportation per capita was greater than in India ($48.8), in Myanmar ($38.9), and in

Vietnam ($29.7); but less than in Japan ($3.7 thousand), in Republic of Korea ($1 471.1), in Kazakhstan ($467.9), and in Russia ($452.0). The growth of transportation in China was greater than in Vietnam (8.3%), in Republic of Korea (7.0%), in Russia (4.7%), and in Japan (1.5%); but less than in Myanmar (18.5%), in India (10.4%), and in Kazakhstan (10.3%).

Comparison with leaders. The sector of transportation in China was less than in the USA ($1.2 trillion), in Japan ($468.5 billion), in Germany ($228.2 billion), in the UK ($215.9 billion), and in France ($185.6 billion). The value of transportation per capita in China was less than in the USA ($4.0 thousand), in Japan ($3.7 thousand), in the UK ($3.6 thousand), in France ($3.0 thousand), and in Germany ($2.8 thousand). The growth of transportation in China was greater than in Germany (3.4%), in the UK (3.1%), in the USA (3.1%), in France (2.7%), and in Japan (1.5%).

The 2010s

The sector of transportation in China was $464.2 billion per year in the 2010s, ranked 3rd in the world, and was on a par with Northern Europe ($460.8 billion). The share in the world was 7.3%, and 24.5% in Asia.

The share of transportation in the economy of China was 4.4% in the 2010s, ranked 196th in the world, and was on a par with Qatar (4.4%).

The Chinese transportation per capita was $331.0 in the 2010s, ranked 126th in the world, and was on a par with South-Eastern Asia ($327.5), Micronesia ($327.4), Guyana ($327.1). The value of transportation per capita in China was less than transportation per capita in the world ($864.8) in 2.6 times, and was less than transportation per capita in Asia ($430.2) by 23.0%.

The growth of transportation in China was 7.5% in the 2010s, ranked 31st in the world, and was on a par with Malaysia (7.5%), the Comoros (7.5%). The growth of transportation in China (7.5%) was greater than growth of transportation in the world (4.0%), was greater than growth of transportation in Asia (4.7%).

Comparison with neighbors. The China's transportation was 3.5 times higher than in India ($132.0 billion), 3.8 times higher than in Russia ($122.2 billion), 4.3 times higher than in Republic of Korea ($107.8 billion), 24.3 times higher than in Kazakhstan ($19.1 billion), 53.5 times higher than in Myanmar ($8.7 billion), and 70.4 times higher than in Vietnam ($6.6 billion); but 12.4% lower than in Japan ($529.8 billion). The value added of transportation per capita in China was 100.0% higher than in Myanmar ($165.5), 3.3 times higher than in India ($101.4), and 4.6 times higher than in Vietnam ($71.5); but 12.5 times lower than in Japan ($4.1 thousand), 6.4 times lower than in South Korea ($2.1 thousand), 3.3 times lower than in Kazakhstan ($1 095.4), and 2.6 times lower than in Russia ($844.4). The growth of transportation in China was greater than in India (6.6%), in Vietnam (6.5%), in Kazakhstan (6.5%), in Republic of Korea (3.7%), in Russia (2.0%), and in Japan (0.81%); but less than in Myanmar (11.8%).

Comparison with leaders. The value of transportation in China was 54.7% higher than in Germany ($300.0 billion), 80.1% higher than in the United Kingdom ($257.7 billion), and 2.0 times higher than in France ($232.0 billion); but 3.9 times lower than in the USA ($1.8 trillion) and 12.4% lower than in Japan ($529.8 billion). The value added of transportation per capita in China was 16.9 times lower than in the United States ($5.6 thousand), 12.5 times lower than in Japan ($4.1 thousand), 11.9 times lower than in the UK ($3.9 thousand), 11.1 times lower than in Germany ($3.7 thousand), and 10.6 times lower than in France ($3.5 thousand). The growth of transportation in China was greater than in the USA (5.1%), in the UK (2.8%), in Germany (2.7%), in France (2.6%), and in Japan (0.81%).

Chapter VIII. Trade

Wholesale, retail trade, restaurants and hotels (ISIC G-H)

The sector of trade in China grew from $11.1 billion per year in the 1970s to $1.2 trillion per year in the 2010s, that is by $1.2 trillion or 107.3 times. The change occurred at $623.0 billion due to a 2.1-fold increase in prices, as also at $554.3 billion due to a 33.4-fold increase in productivity, as well as at $5.9 billion due to the rise in population. The average annual growth in trade is 9.5%. The minimum value of trade was in 1970 at $7.7 billion. The maximum value of trade was in 2019 at $1.6 trillion.

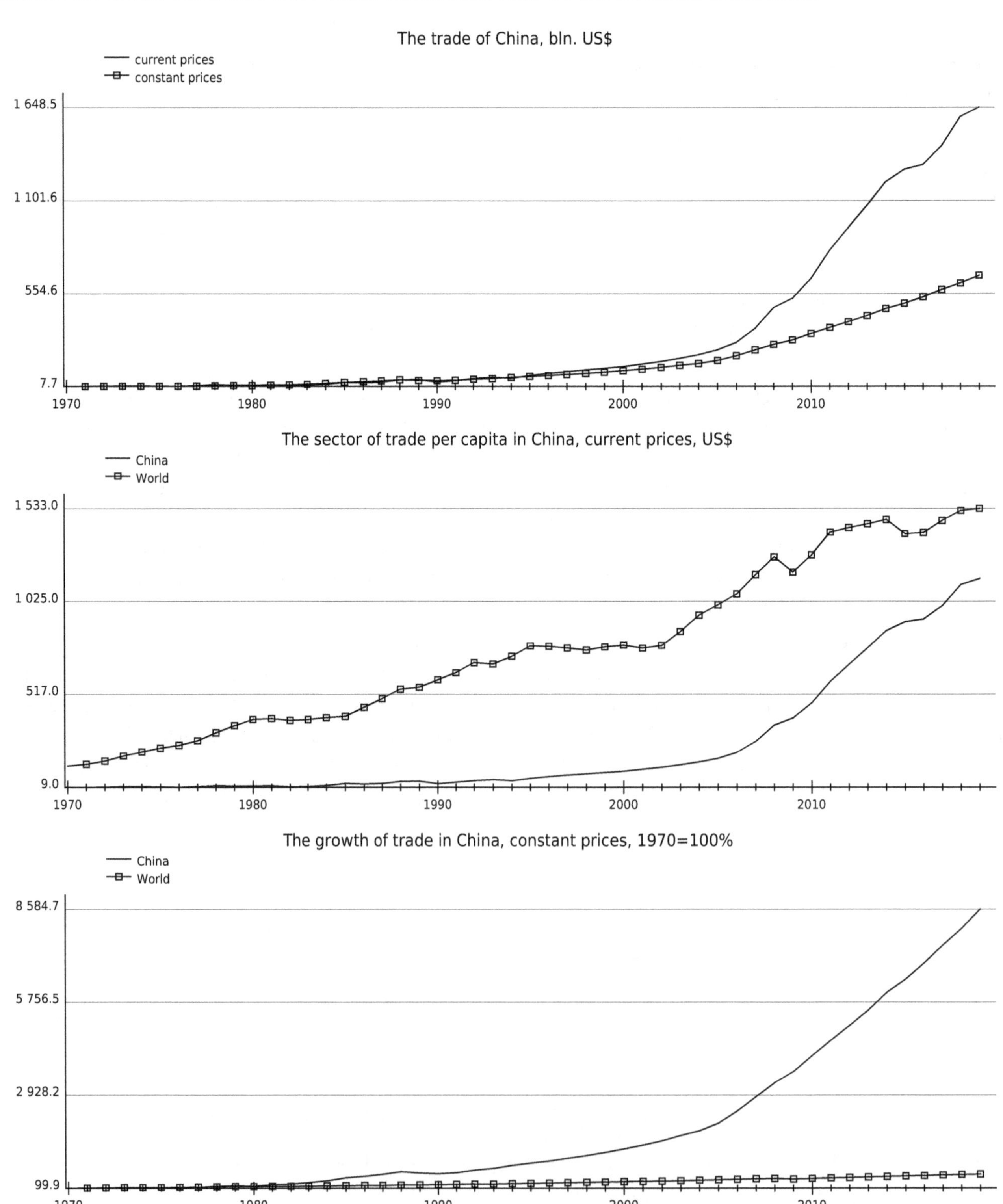

The 1970s

The value of trade in China was $11.1 billion per year in the 1970s, ranked 13th in the world, and was on a par with Switzerland ($11.0 billion). The share in the world was 1.2%, and 7.1% in Asia.

The share of trade in the economy of China was 7.1% in the 1970s, ranked 169th in the world, and was on a par with Ghana (7.1%).

The value added of trade per capita in China was $12.2 in the 1970s, ranked 174th in the world. The sector of trade per capita in China was less than trade per capita in the world ($221.0) in 18.1 times, and was less than trade per capita in Asia ($67.4) in 5.5 times.

The growth of trade in China was 6.1% in the 1970s, ranked 65th in the world, and was on a par with Luxembourg (6.0%), Colombia (6.1%), Central America (6.1%). The growth of trade in China (6.1%) was greater than growth of trade in the world (4.5%), was less than growth of trade in Asia (7.7%).

Comparison with neighbors. The value added of trade in China was greater than in India ($5.8 billion), in South Korea ($4.1 billion), in Myanmar ($1.0 billion), and in Vietnam ($553.4 million); but less than in Japan ($90.3 billion) and in the USSR ($62.3 billion). The sector of trade per capita in China was greater than in Vietnam ($11.5) and in India ($9.4); but less than in Japan ($811.1), in the USSR ($247.1), in Republic of Korea ($117.6), and in Myanmar ($33.3). The growth of trade in China was greater than in the USSR (5.2%), in Vietnam (4.7%), in India (4.1%), and in Myanmar (3.4%); but less than in South Korea (8.5%) and in Japan (8.2%).

Comparison with leaders. The China's trade was less than in the United States ($278.3 billion), in Japan ($90.3 billion), in the USSR ($62.3 billion), in Germany ($61.1 billion), and in France ($40.9 billion). The trade per capita in China was less than in the United States ($1 275.1), in Japan ($811.1), in Germany ($775.5), in France ($762.4), and in the USSR ($247.1). The growth of trade in China was greater than in the USSR (5.2%), in France (3.9%), in the United States (3.9%), and in Germany (3.0%); but less than in Japan (8.2%).

The 1980s

The sector of trade in China was $26.8 billion per year in the 1980s, ranked 11th in the world. The share in the world was 1.3%, and 5.7% in Asia.

The share of trade in the economy of China was 8.1% in the 1980s, ranked 168th in the world.

The trade per capita in China was $25.0 in the 1980s, ranked 175th in the world, and was on a par with Bhutan ($25.2), Cambodia ($25.2). The value added of trade per capita in China was less than trade per capita in the world ($437.7) in 17.5 times, and was less than trade per capita in Asia ($166.8) in 6.7 times.

The growth of trade in China was 12.7% in the 1980s, ranked 3rd in the world. The growth of trade in China (12.7%) was greater than growth of trade in the world (3.3%), was greater than growth of trade in Asia (5.8%).

Comparison with neighbors. The value added of trade in China was greater than in India ($16.8 billion), in Republic of Korea ($16.5 billion), in Myanmar ($1.4 billion), and in Vietnam ($539.1 million); but less than in Japan ($277.3 billion) and in the USSR ($112.3 billion). The sector of trade per capita in China was greater than in India ($21.7) and in Vietnam ($8.9); but less than in Japan ($2.3 thousand), in Republic of Korea ($409.3), in the USSR ($408.1), and in Myanmar ($36.8). The growth of trade in China was greater than in South Korea (8.1%), in India (6.1%), in Japan (4.9%), in Vietnam (4.6%), in Myanmar (0.18%), and in the USSR (-0.62%).

Comparison with leaders. The sector of trade in China was less than in the United States ($653.3 billion), in Japan ($277.3 billion), in Germany ($116.7 billion), in the USSR ($112.3 billion), and in Italy ($95.7 billion). The value added of trade per capita in China was less than in the USA ($2.7 thousand), in Japan ($2.3 thousand), in Italy ($1 684.2), in Germany ($1 496.0), and in the USSR ($408.1). The growth of trade in China was greater than in Japan (4.9%), in the United States (4.4%), in Italy (2.3%), in Germany (1.8%), and in the USSR (-0.62%).

The 1990s

The value added of trade in China was $71.6 billion per year in the 1990s, ranked 11th in the world. The share in the world was 1.7%, and 6.1% in Asia.

The share of trade in the economy of China was 10.0% in the 1990s, ranked 170th in the world, and was on a par with Macedonia (9.9%), Angola (9.9%).

The trade per capita in China was $58.1 in the 1990s, ranked 169th in the world, and was on a par with Benin ($57.9). The China's trade per capita was less than trade per capita in the world ($721.8) in 12.4 times, and was less than trade per capita in Asia ($337.1) in 5.8 times.

The growth of trade in China was 7.7% in the 1990s, ranked 16th in the world. The growth of trade in China (7.7%) was greater than growth of trade in the world (3.5%), was greater than growth of trade in Asia (4.9%).

Comparison with neighbors. The value of trade in China was greater than in Republic of Korea ($50.0 billion), in India ($28.0 billion), in Vietnam ($3.4 billion), in Kazakhstan ($3.0 billion), and in Myanmar ($1.8 billion); but less than in Japan ($713.2 billion) and in Russia ($73.9 billion). The sector of trade per capita in China was greater than in Vietnam ($45.5), in Myanmar ($40.1), and in India ($29.3); but less than in Japan ($5.7 thousand), in South Korea ($1 111.2), in Russia ($499.6), and in Kazakhstan ($187.5). The growth of trade in China was greater than in India (7.6%), in Vietnam (6.5%), in South Korea (5.8%), in Myanmar (5.6%), in Japan (3.8%), in Russia (-1.9%), and in Kazakhstan (-3.0%).

Comparison with leaders. The value added of trade in China was less than in the United States ($1.2 trillion), in Japan ($713.2 billion), in Germany ($243.7 billion), in Italy ($185.6 billion), and in France ($177.0 billion). The value added of trade per capita in China was less than in Japan ($5.7 thousand), in the USA ($4.4 thousand), in Italy ($3.3 thousand), in Germany ($3.0 thousand), and in France ($3.0 thousand). The growth of trade in China was greater than in the United States (4.3%), in Japan (3.8%), in Germany (2.5%), in France (2.4%), and in Italy (1.9%).

The 2000s

The sector of trade in China was $262.0 billion per year in the 2000s, ranked 5th in the world, and was on a par with Eastern Europe ($263.3 billion), France ($256.9 billion). The share in the world was 4.1%, and 15.1% in Asia.

The share of trade in the economy of China was 10.1% in the 2000s, ranked 184th in the world, and was on a par with Chile (10.2%).

The value added of trade per capita in China was $197.5 in the 2000s, ranked 148th in the world, and was on a par with the Comoros ($200.5), Central Asia ($194.5). The Chinese trade per capita was less than trade per capita in the world ($990.3) in 5.0 times, and was less than trade per capita in Asia ($438.7) in 2.2 times.

The growth of trade in China was 11.9% in the 2000s, ranked 7th in the world, and was on a par with Macao (11.8%), Tajikistan (11.8%), Nigeria (12.0%). The growth of trade in China (11.9%) was greater than growth of trade in the world (2.7%), was greater than growth of trade in Asia (4.5%).

Comparison with neighbors. The trade of China was greater than in Russia ($143.6 billion), in South Korea ($85.1 billion), in India ($78.2 billion), in Vietnam ($9.7 billion), in Kazakhstan ($8.2 billion), and in Myanmar ($3.5 billion); but less than in Japan ($771.8 billion). The trade per capita in China was greater than in Vietnam ($116.0), in Myanmar ($71.6), and in India ($68.7); but less than in Japan ($6.0 thousand), in Republic of Korea ($1 754.9), in Russia ($995.4), and in Kazakhstan ($530.2). The growth of trade in China was greater than in Myanmar (11.5%), in Russia (8.4%), in Kazakhstan (8.2%), in Vietnam (7.7%), in India (7.0%), in South Korea (2.6%), and in Japan (-0.77%).

Comparison with leaders. The value added of trade in China was greater than in France ($256.9 billion); but less than in the United States ($1.9 trillion), in Japan ($771.8 billion), in Germany ($296.0 billion), and in the United Kingdom ($293.5 billion). The sector of trade per capita in China was less than in the USA ($6.4 thousand), in Japan ($6.0 thousand), in the UK ($4.9 thousand), in France

($4.1 thousand), and in Germany ($3.6 thousand). The growth of trade in China was greater than in Germany (1.7%), in the United Kingdom (1.3%), in France (1.2%), in the United States (1.1%), and in Japan (-0.77%).

The 2010s

The China's trade was $1.2 trillion per year in the 2010s, ranked 2nd in the world. The share in the world was 11.3%, and 33.0% in Asia.

The share of trade in the economy of China was 11.4% in the 2010s, ranked 169th in the world, and was on a par with Australia (11.4%), Eritrea (11.4%), Germany (11.3%).

The value added of trade per capita in China was $851.7 in the 2010s, ranked 106th in the world, and was on a par with Southern Africa ($853.8). The value of trade per capita in China was less than trade per capita in the world ($1 436.8) by 40.7%, and was greater than trade per capita in Asia ($821.1) by 3.7%.

The growth of trade in China was 8.9% in the 2010s, ranked 13th in the world. The growth of trade in China (8.9%) was greater than growth of trade in the world (3.3%), was greater than growth of trade in Asia (5.6%).

Comparison with neighbors. The value of trade in China was 37.4% higher than in Japan ($869.5 billion), 4.3 times higher than in Russia ($277.2 billion), 5.1 times higher than in India ($232.5 billion), 8.4 times higher than in South Korea ($141.9 billion), 38.6 times higher than in Kazakhstan ($30.9 billion), 45.6 times higher than in Vietnam ($26.2 billion), and 94.6 times higher than in Myanmar ($12.6 billion). The trade per capita in China was 3.0 times higher than in Vietnam ($283.8), 3.5 times higher than in Myanmar ($240.9), and 4.8 times higher than in India ($178.6); but 8.0 times lower than in Japan ($6.8 thousand), 3.3 times lower than in Republic of Korea ($2.8 thousand), 2.2 times lower than in Russia ($1 914.6), and 2.1 times lower than in Kazakhstan ($1 775.1). The growth of trade in China was greater than in Kazakhstan (7.6%), in Myanmar (6.6%), in Vietnam (4.2%), in Republic of Korea (3.1%), in Russia (1.7%), and in Japan (0.77%); but less than in India (9.7%).

Comparison with leaders. The value of trade in China was 37.4% higher than in Japan ($869.5 billion), 3.2 times higher than in Germany ($372.6 billion), 3.6 times higher than in the United Kingdom ($330.0 billion), and 3.8 times higher than in France ($315.4 billion); but 2.2 times lower than in the United States ($2.6 trillion). The value of trade per capita in China was 9.6 times lower than in the USA ($8.2 thousand), 8.0 times lower than in Japan ($6.8 thousand), 5.9 times lower than in the United Kingdom ($5.0 thousand), 5.6 times lower than in France ($4.8 thousand), and 5.3 times lower than in Germany ($4.6 thousand). The growth of trade in China was greater than in the UK (2.8%), in the USA (2.3%), in Germany (2.0%), in France (1.9%), and in Japan (0.77%).

Chapter IX. Services

(ISIC J-P)

The value added of services in China enlarged from $17.8 billion per year in the 1970s to $3.5 trillion per year in the 2010s, that is by $3.5 trillion or 198.8 times. The change occurred at $2.5 trillion due to a 3.4-fold increase in prices, as also at $1.0 trillion due to a 37.9-fold increase in productivity, as well as at $9.5 billion due to the increase in population. The average annual growth in services is 9.9%. The minimum value of services was in 1970 at $10.9 billion. The maximum value of services was in 2019 at $5.4 trillion.

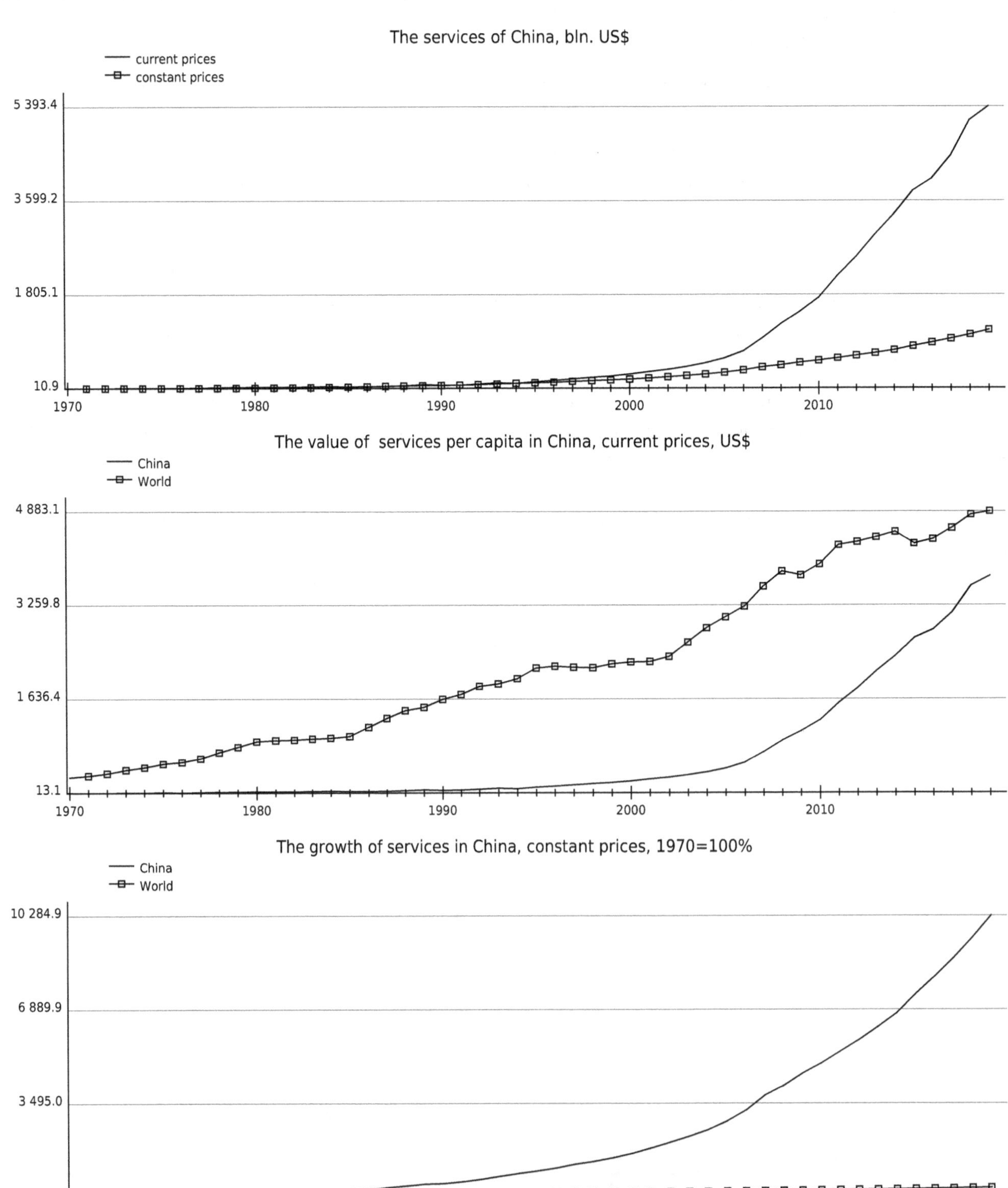

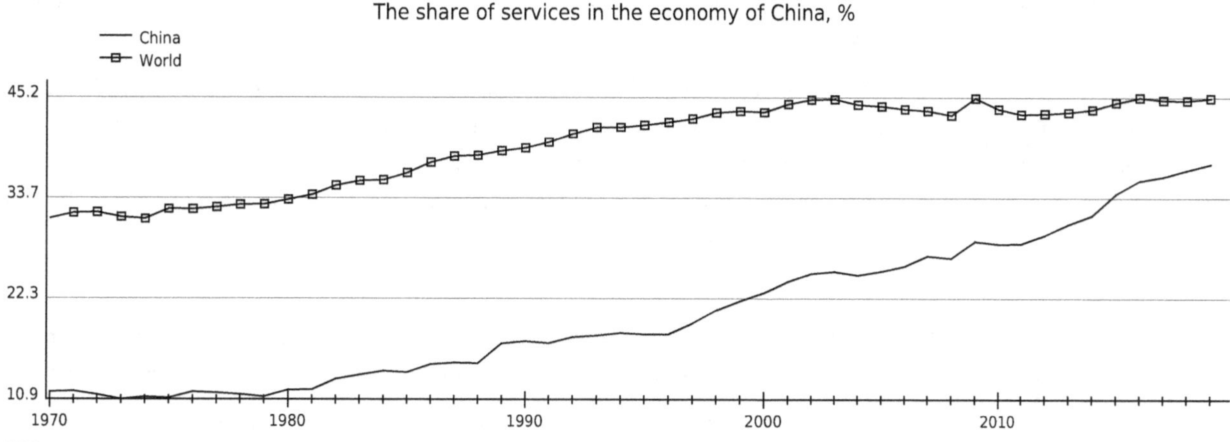

The 1970s

The value of services in China was $17.8 billion per year in the 1970s, ranked 19th in the world. The share in the world was 0.87%, and 6.3% in Asia.

The share of services in the economy of China was 11.4% in the 1970s, ranked 178th in the world.

The value added of services per capita in China was $19.5 in the 1970s, ranked 176th in the world, and was on a par with Ethiopia ($19.8). The value of services per capita in China was less than services per capita in the world ($506.9) in 26.0 times, and was less than services per capita in Asia ($121.6) in 6.2 times.

The growth of services in China was 5.5% in the 1970s, ranked 80th in the world, and was on a par with Greece (5.5%), Africa (5.5%), Central America (5.5%). The growth of services in China (5.5%) was greater than growth of services in the world (4.1%), was less than growth of services in Asia (6.5%).

Comparison with neighbors. The services of China were greater than in Republic of Korea ($4.9 billion), in Vietnam ($1.2 billion), and in Myanmar ($454.1 million); but less than in the USSR ($168.3 billion), in Japan ($153.8 billion), and in India ($22.5 billion). The services per capita in China were greater than in Myanmar ($15.0); but less than in Japan ($1 381.3), in the USSR ($667.3), in Republic of Korea ($140.3), in India ($36.4), and in Vietnam ($25.9). The growth of services in China was greater than in Myanmar (5.2%), in Vietnam (4.7%), in India (4.3%), and in the USSR (0.90%); but less than in South Korea (7.5%) and in Japan (5.9%).

Comparison with leaders. The sector of services in China was less than in the USA ($674.4 billion), in the USSR ($168.3 billion), in Japan ($153.8 billion), in Germany ($150.2 billion), and in France ($121.8 billion). The value added of services per capita in China was less than in the USA ($3.1 thousand), in France ($2.3 thousand), in Germany ($1 907.6), in Japan ($1 381.3), and in the USSR ($667.3). The growth of services in China was greater than in Germany (4.8%), in France (3.9%), in the USA (3.3%), and in the USSR (0.90%); but less than in Japan (5.9%).

The 1980s

The value added of services in China was $47.3 billion per year in the 1980s, ranked 18th in the world, and was on a par with Western Africa ($46.2 billion). The share in the world was 0.88%, and 4.7% in Asia.

The share of services in the economy of China was 14.3% in the 1980s, ranked 174th in the world.

The value of services per capita in China was $44.1 in the 1980s, ranked 173rd in the world, and was on a par with Bangladesh ($44.2). The China's services per capita were less than services per capita in the world ($1 115.5) in 25.3 times, and were less than services per capita in Asia ($351.5) in 8.0 times.

The growth of services in China was 13.7% in the 1980s, ranked 5th in the world. The growth of services in China (13.7%) was greater than growth of services in the world (3.3%), was greater than growth of services in Asia (5.3%).

Comparison with neighbors. The value of services in China was greater than in Republic of Korea ($28.9 billion), in Vietnam ($1.2 billion), and in Myanmar ($607.6 million); but less than in Japan ($619.9 billion), in the USSR ($231.9 billion), and in India ($51.5 billion). The value added of services per capita in China was greater than in Vietnam ($19.8) and in Myanmar ($16.2); but less than in Japan ($5.1 thousand), in the USSR ($842.7), in Republic of Korea ($715.3), and in India ($66.3). The growth of services in China was greater than in Republic of Korea (9.4%), in India (6.7%), in the USSR (6.3%), in Japan (4.8%), in Vietnam (4.8%), and in Myanmar (4.4%).

Comparison with leaders. The value of services in China was less than in the United States ($1.9 trillion), in Japan ($619.9 billion), in Germany ($362.2 billion), in France ($294.5 billion), and in the UK ($265.4 billion). The sector of services per capita in China was less than in the United States ($7.8 thousand), in France ($5.2 thousand), in Japan ($5.1 thousand), in the United Kingdom ($4.7 thousand), and in Germany ($4.6 thousand). The growth of services in China was greater than in Japan (4.8%), in the United Kingdom (3.3%), in Germany (3.1%), in the United States (2.8%), and in France (2.3%).

The 1990s

The services of China were $138.4 billion per year in the 1990s, ranked 14th in the world, and were on a par with Mexico ($138.9 billion), Republic of Korea ($139.6 billion), South-Eastern Asia ($139.8 billion). The share in the world was 1.2%, and 5.5% in Asia.

The share of services in the economy of China was 19.3% in the 1990s, ranked 177th in the world, and was on a par with Angola (19.3%).

The value of services per capita in China was $112.3 in the 1990s, ranked 164th in the world, and was on a par with Middle Africa ($112.9), Equatorial Guinea ($110.4), Yemen ($109.9). The sector of services per capita in China was less than services per capita in the world ($2 014.6) in 17.9 times, and was less than services per capita in Asia ($732.9) in 6.5 times.

The growth of services in China was 10% in the 1990s, ranked 7th in the world, and was on a par with Vietnam (10.0%). The growth of services in China (10.0%) was greater than growth of services in the world (2.7%), was greater than growth of services in Asia (4.5%).

Comparison with neighbors. The Chinese services were greater than in India ($83.4 billion), in Russia ($71.4 billion), in Kazakhstan ($7.4 billion), in Vietnam ($5.2 billion), and in Myanmar ($300.8 million); but less than in Japan ($1.6 trillion) and in Republic of Korea ($139.6 billion). The China's services per capita were greater than in India ($87.3), in Vietnam ($70.1), and in Myanmar ($6.9); but less than in Japan ($12.8 thousand), in Republic of Korea ($3.1 thousand), in Russia ($482.5), and in Kazakhstan ($469.6). The growth of services in China was greater than in India (7.7%), in South Korea (7.1%), in Myanmar (5.5%), in Japan (1.7%), in Russia (-1.2%), and in Kazakhstan (-5.1%); but less than in Vietnam (10.0%).

Comparison with leaders. The value of services in China was less than in the USA ($3.8 trillion), in Japan ($1.6 trillion), in Germany ($908.0 billion), in France ($628.2 billion), and in the United Kingdom ($592.3 billion). The sector of services per capita in China was less than in the USA ($14.4 thousand), in Japan ($12.8 thousand), in Germany ($11.3 thousand), in France ($10.6 thousand), and in the United Kingdom ($10.2 thousand). The growth of services in China was greater than in Germany (3.2%), in the UK (3.0%), in the United States (2.3%), in Japan (1.7%), and in France (1.6%).

The 2000s

The Chinese services were $686.4 billion per year in the 2000s, ranked 7th in the world. The share in the world was 3.5%, and 16.2% in Asia.

The share of services in the economy of China was 26.5% in the 2000s, ranked 144th in the world, and was on a par with Saudi Arabia (26.3%).

The value of services per capita in China was $517.4 in the 2000s, ranked 135th in the world, and was on a par with Ukraine ($507.4). The China's services per capita were less than services per capita in the world ($3 011.2) in 5.8 times, and were less than services per capita in Asia ($1 071.6) in 2.1 times.

The growth of services in China was 11.6% in the 2000s, ranked 6th in the world. The growth of services in China (11.6%) was greater than growth of services in the world (2.9%), was greater than growth of services in Asia (5.5%).

Comparison with neighbors. The China's services were greater than in Republic of Korea ($300.2 billion), in India ($233.2 billion), in Russia ($195.9 billion), in Kazakhstan ($17.8 billion), in Vietnam ($14.0 billion), and in Myanmar ($541.1 million); but less than in Japan ($2.0 trillion). The value of services per capita in China was greater than in India ($204.9), in Vietnam ($167.3), and in Myanmar ($11.1); but less than in Japan ($15.3 thousand), in South Korea ($6.2 thousand), in Russia ($1 357.8), and in Kazakhstan ($1 157.8). The growth of services in China was greater than in Myanmar (11.0%), in Kazakhstan (8.5%), in India (7.1%), in Vietnam (6.0%), in South Korea (4.8%), in Russia (4.3%), and in Japan (1.2%).

Comparison with leaders. The value of services in China was less than in the United States ($6.7 trillion), in Japan ($2.0 trillion), in Germany ($1.2 trillion), in the UK ($1.1 trillion), and in France ($997.0 billion). The sector of services per capita in China was less than in the United States ($22.9 thousand), in the UK ($18.0 thousand), in France ($15.9 thousand), in Japan ($15.3 thousand), and in Germany ($15.0 thousand). The growth of services in China was greater than in the UK (2.7%), in the USA (2.0%), in France (1.5%), in Japan (1.2%), and in Germany (0.57%).

The 2010s

The Chinese services were $3.5 trillion per year in the 2010s, ranked 2nd in the world. The share in the world was 10.8%, and 37.6% in Asia.

The share of services in the economy of China was 33.8% in the 2010s, ranked 113th in the world, and was on a par with India (33.7%), Mexico (33.8%), Ecuador (33.5%).

The sector of services per capita in China was $2 529.2 in the 2010s, ranked 96th in the world, and was on a par with Malaysia ($2.5 thousand), South Africa ($2.5 thousand), Venezuela ($2.5 thousand). The value added of services per capita in China was less than services per capita in the world ($4 467.8) by 43.4%, and was greater than services per capita in Asia ($2 137.6) by 18.3%.

The growth of services in China was 8.4% in the 2010s, ranked 7th in the world. The growth of services in China (8.4%) was greater than growth of services in the world (2.7%), was greater than growth of services in Asia (5.4%).

Comparison with neighbors. The value added of services in China was 56.0% higher than in Japan ($2.3 trillion), 5.2 times higher than in India ($681.5 billion), 6.1 times higher than in Russia ($577.3 billion), 6.4 times higher than in Republic of Korea ($553.7 billion), 69.6 times higher than in Kazakhstan ($51.0 billion), 83.4 times higher than in Vietnam ($42.5 billion), and 900.7 times higher than in Myanmar ($3.9 billion). The value added of services per capita in China was 4.8 times higher than in India ($523.5), 5.5 times higher than in Vietnam ($461.0), and 33.7 times higher than in Myanmar ($75.2); but 7.0 times lower than in Japan ($17.8 thousand), 4.3 times lower than in Republic of Korea ($10.9 thousand), 36.6% lower than in Russia ($4.0 thousand), and 13.5% lower than in Kazakhstan ($2.9 thousand). The growth of services in China was greater than in India (7.8%), in Vietnam (5.9%), in Kazakhstan (3.8%), in Republic of Korea (3.4%), in Russia (1.5%), and in Japan (0.99%); but less than in Myanmar (10.6%).

Comparison with leaders. The sector of services in China was 56.0% higher than in Japan ($2.3 trillion), 2.2 times higher than in Germany ($1.6 trillion), 2.6 times higher than in the UK ($1.4 trillion), and 2.6 times higher than in France ($1.3 trillion); but 2.8 times lower than in the United States ($10.0 trillion). The value added of services per capita in China was 12.3 times lower than in the United States ($31.2 thousand), 8.2 times lower than in the UK ($20.7 thousand), 8.0 times lower than in France ($20.2 thousand), 7.8 times lower than in Germany ($19.6 thousand), and 7.0 times lower than in Japan ($17.8 thousand). The growth of services in China was greater than in the USA (1.8%), in the UK (1.7%), in France (1.4%), in Germany (1.2%), and in Japan (0.99%).

Part III. External relations

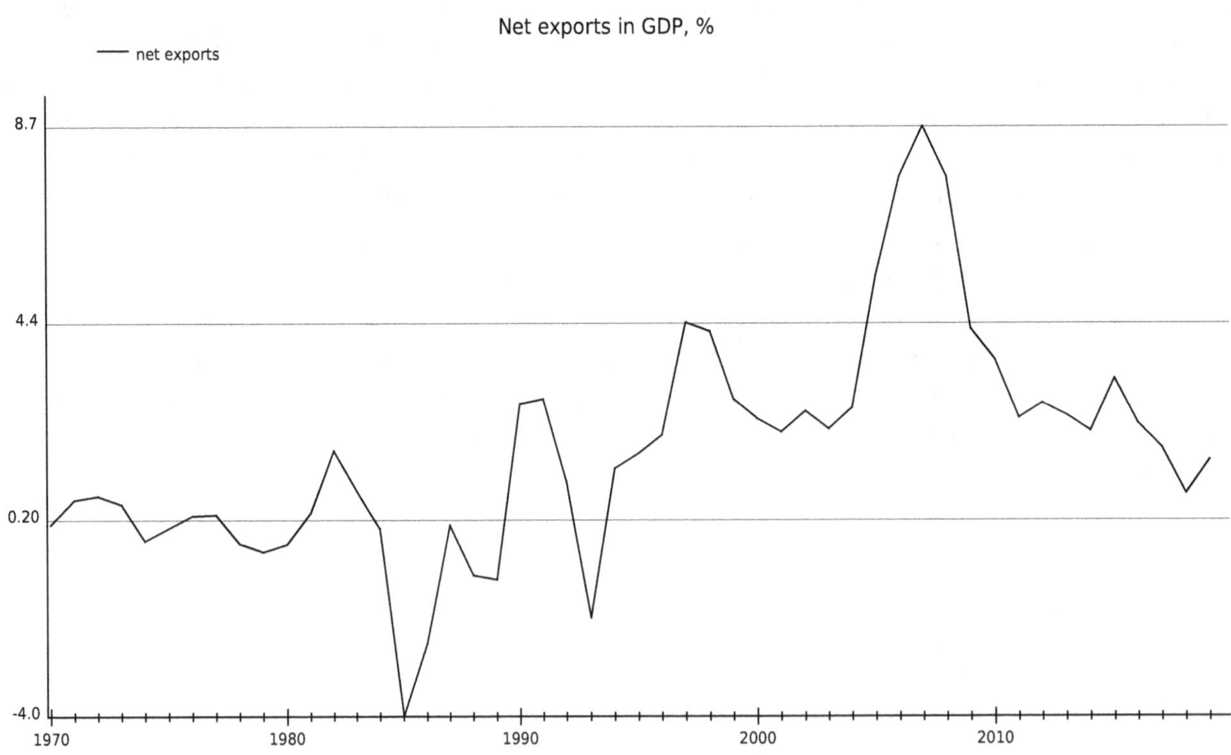

Chapter X. Exports

Exports of goods and services

The exports of China enlarged from $7.9 billion per year in the 1970s to $2.3 trillion per year in the 2010s, that is by $2.3 trillion or 289.4 times. The change occurred at $727.4 billion due to a 1.5-fold increase in prices, as also at $1.6 trillion due to a 128.8-fold increase in per capita rate, as well as at $4.2 billion due to the growth in population. The average annual growth in exports is 13.6%. The minimum value of exports was in 1970 at $2.7 billion. The maximum value of exports was in 2019 at $2.7 trillion.

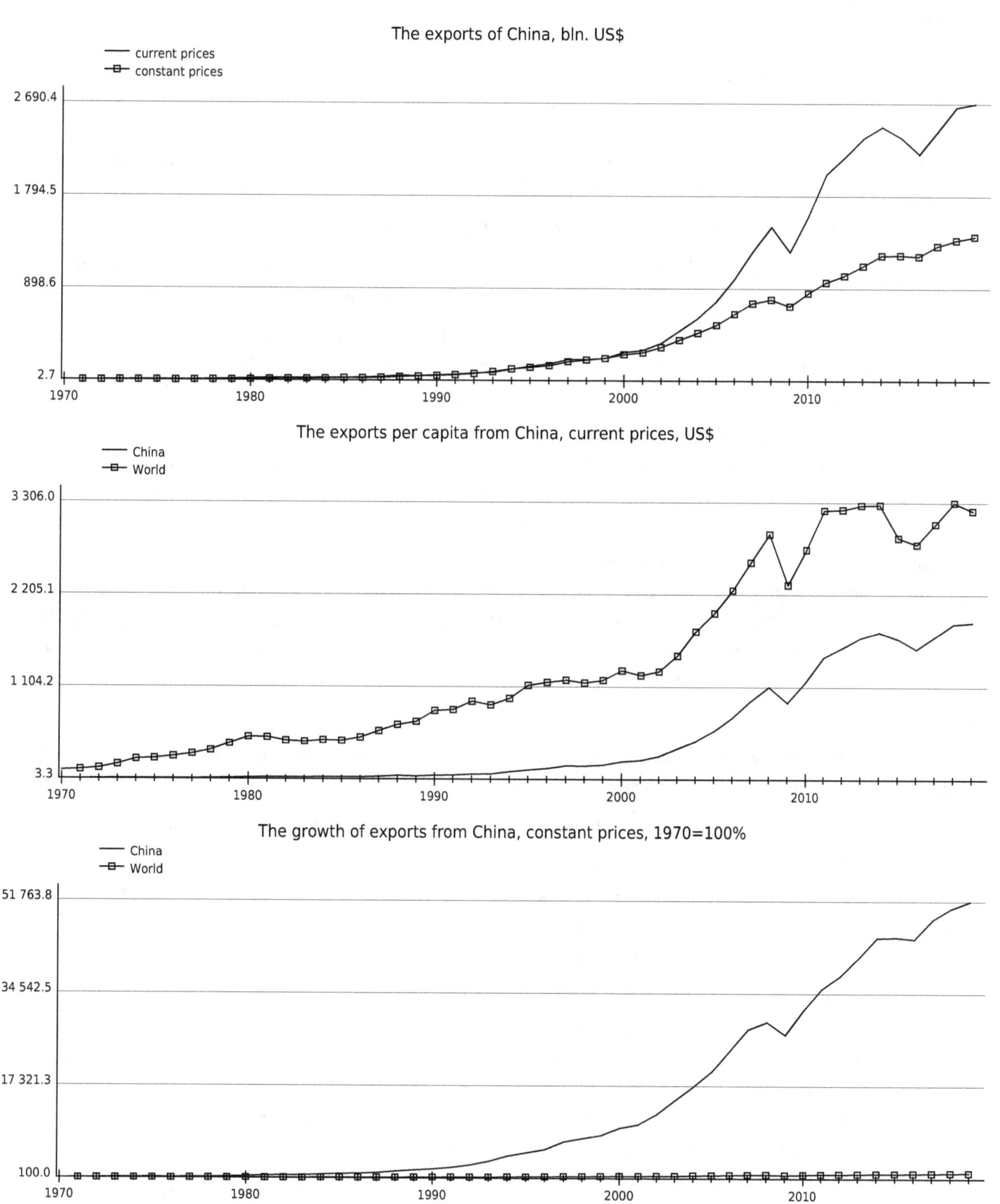

The exports of China, bln. US$

The exports per capita from China, current prices, US$

The growth of exports from China, constant prices, 1970=100%

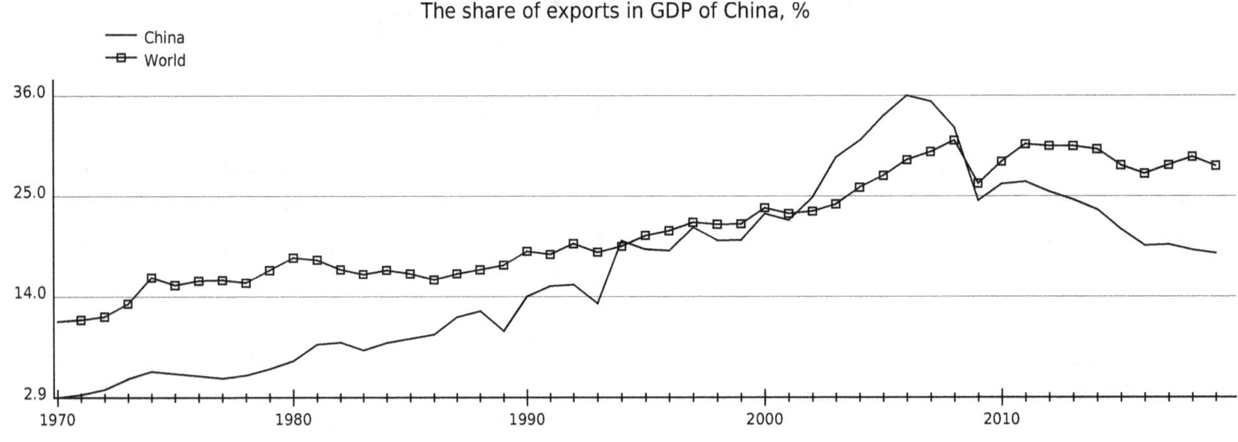

The 1970s

The value of exports from China was $7.9 billion per year in the 1970s, ranked 26th in the world, and was on a par with Singapore ($8.0 billion). The share in the world was 0.81%, and 3.8% from Asia.

The share of exports in GDP of China was 5.1% in the 1970s, ranked 178th in the world.

The exports per capita from China were $8.7 in the 1970s, ranked 179th in the world. The exports per capita from China were less than exports per capita in the world ($242.1) in 27.9 times, and were less than exports per capita from Asia ($90.8) in 10.5 times.

The growth of exports from China was 15% in the 1970s, ranked 9th in the world. The growth of exports from China (15.0%) was greater than growth of exports in the world (6.5%), was greater than growth of exports from Asia (7.9%).

Comparison with neighbors. The value of exports from China was greater than from Republic of Korea ($6.3 billion), from India ($5.5 billion), from Vietnam ($1.1 billion), and from Myanmar ($219.6 million); but less than from Japan ($64.1 billion). The value of exports per capita from China was greater than from Myanmar ($7.2); but less than from Japan ($575.8), from South Korea ($180.6), from Vietnam ($23.4), and from India ($9.0). The growth of exports from China was greater than from Japan (8.6%), from India (8.0%), from Vietnam (4.7%), and from Myanmar (2.1%); but less than from South Korea (24.0%).

Comparison with leaders. The value of exports from China was less than from the USA ($128.0 billion), from Germany ($82.9 billion), from France ($64.3 billion), from Japan ($64.1 billion), and from the United Kingdom ($61.3 billion). The China's exports per capita were less than from France ($1 199.1), from the United Kingdom ($1 094.1), from Germany ($1 052.2), from the USA ($586.5), and from Japan ($575.8). The growth of exports from China was greater than from Japan (8.6%), from France (7.8%), from the United States (6.8%), from Germany (5.1%), and from the United Kingdom (5.0%).

The 1980s

The value of exports from China was $31.8 billion per year in the 1980s, ranked 19th in the world, and was on a par with Australia ($32.2 billion). The share in the world was 1.2%, and 4.9% from Asia.

The share of exports in GDP of China was 9.7% in the 1980s, ranked 163rd in the world, and was on a par with Guinea-Bissau (9.7%), Northern America (9.7%), Brazil (9.7%).

The China's exports per capita were $29.7 in the 1980s, ranked 166th in the world. The China's exports per capita were less than exports per capita in the world ($529.9) in 17.8 times, and were less than exports per capita from Asia ($229.0) in 7.7 times.

The growth of exports from China was 16.5% in the 1980s, ranked 4th in the world. The growth of exports from China (16.5%) was greater than growth of exports in the world (3.8%), was greater than growth of exports from Asia (4.1%).

Comparison with neighbors. The China's exports were greater than from India ($14.3 billion), from Vietnam ($1.1 billion), and from Myanmar ($298.0 million); but less than from Japan ($210.6 billion) and from Republic of Korea ($36.3 billion). The Chinese exports per capita were greater than from India ($18.5), from Vietnam ($17.9), and from Myanmar ($7.9); but less than from Japan ($1 736.5) and from South Korea ($898.1). The growth of exports from China was greater than from South Korea (11.6%), from Japan (6.7%), from India (4.7%), from Vietnam (3.8%), and from Myanmar (3.3%).

Comparison with leaders. The exports of China were less than from the United States ($338.6 billion), from Japan ($210.6 billion), from Germany ($208.1 billion), from France ($155.9 billion), and from the United Kingdom ($155.0 billion). The value of exports per capita from China was less than from France ($2.8 thousand), from the United Kingdom ($2.7 thousand), from Germany ($2.7 thousand), from Japan ($1 736.5), and from the United States ($1 413.8). The growth of exports from China was greater than from Japan (6.7%), from the United States (5.7%), from Germany (4.7%), from France (4.0%), and from the UK (3.0%).

The 1990s

The Chinese exports were $132.9 billion per year in the 1990s, ranked 11th in the world, and were on a par with Russia ($130.4 billion). The share in the world was 2.3%, and 8.4% from Asia.

The share of exports in GDP of China was 18.5% in the 1990s, ranked 161st in the world, and was on a par with Iran (18.5%), Madagascar (18.6%).

The exports per capita from China were $107.8 in the 1990s, ranked 168th in the world. The Chinese exports per capita were less than exports per capita in the world ($1 029.5) in 9.6 times, and were less than exports per capita from Asia ($456.7) in 4.2 times.

The growth of exports from China was 17.5% in the 1990s, ranked 7th in the world. The growth of exports from China (17.5%) was greater than growth of exports in the world (6.9%), was greater than growth of exports from Asia (8.1%).

Comparison with neighbors. The China's exports were greater than from Russia ($130.4 billion), from Republic of Korea ($121.2 billion), from India ($36.1 billion), from Kazakhstan ($8.5 billion), from Vietnam ($7.2 billion), and from Myanmar ($1.1 billion); but less than from Japan ($418.7 billion). The value of exports per capita from China was greater than from Vietnam ($97.0), from India ($37.8), and from Myanmar ($24.7); but less than from Japan ($3.3 thousand), from South Korea ($2.7 thousand), from Russia ($881.8), and from Kazakhstan ($536.4). The growth of exports from China was greater than from Vietnam (15.6%), from South Korea (13.5%), from Myanmar (13.1%), from Russia (12.1%), from India (11.7%), from Japan (4.2%), and from Kazakhstan (-4.6%).

Comparison with leaders. The Chinese exports were less than from the USA ($773.6 billion), from Germany ($509.0 billion), from Japan ($418.7 billion), from France ($329.8 billion), and from the United Kingdom ($324.3 billion). The exports per capita from China were less than from Germany ($6.3 thousand), from the UK ($5.6 thousand), from France ($5.6 thousand), from Japan ($3.3 thousand), and from the United States ($2.9 thousand). The growth of exports from China was greater than from the United States (7.2%), from France (6.5%), from Germany (6.0%), from the UK (5.7%), and from Japan (4.2%).

The 2000s

The exports of China were $780.2 billion per year in the 2000s, ranked 3rd in the world, and were on a par with South-Eastern Asia ($767.6 billion). The share in the world was 6.2%, and 19.5% from Asia.

The structure of exports: primary products (4.3%), resource-based manufactures (8.2%), low technology manufactures (32.4%), medium technology manufactures (22.5%), and high technology manufactures (32.2%).

China exported goods to the USA (19.7%), Hong Kong (15.4%), Japan (10.2%), South Korea (4.7%), Germany (4.1%) and other countries (45.9%).

The share of exports in GDP of China was 30.1% in the 2000s, ranked 126th in the world, and was on a par with Afghanistan (30.1%).

The Chinese exports per capita were $588.1 in the 2000s, ranked 138th in the world, and were on a par with Colombia ($591.6). The value of exports per capita from China was less than exports per capita in the world ($1 933.7) in 3.3 times, and was less than exports per capita from Asia ($1 011.8) by 41.9%.

The growth of exports from China was 12.7% in the 2000s, ranked 15th in the world, and was on a par with Djibouti (12.7%). The growth of exports from China (12.7%) was greater than growth of exports in the world (4.8%), was greater than growth of exports from Asia (7.5%).

Comparison with neighbors. The exports of China were greater than from Japan ($626.3 billion), from Republic of Korea ($313.8 billion), from Russia ($256.1 billion), from India ($159.3 billion), from Vietnam ($38.3 billion), from Kazakhstan ($31.8 billion), and from Myanmar ($4.4 billion). The value of exports per capita from China was greater than from Vietnam ($458.5), from India ($140.0), and from Myanmar ($90.4); but less than from Republic of Korea ($6.5 thousand), from Japan ($4.9 thousand), from Kazakhstan ($2.1 thousand), and from Russia ($1 774.6). The growth of exports from China was greater than from Vietnam (11.1%), from Republic of Korea (10.0%), from Russia (6.3%), from Kazakhstan (6.2%), from Myanmar (4.4%), and from Japan (3.5%); but less than from India

(13.8%).

Comparison with leaders. The exports of China were greater than from Japan ($626.3 billion), from the United Kingdom ($591.1 billion), and from France ($570.1 billion); but less than from the USA ($1.3 trillion) and from Germany ($1.0 trillion). The value of exports per capita from China was less than from Germany ($12.8 thousand), from the United Kingdom ($9.8 thousand), from France ($9.1 thousand), from Japan ($4.9 thousand), and from the USA ($4.5 thousand). The growth of exports from China was greater than from Germany (5.0%), from Japan (3.5%), from the USA (3.3%), from the United Kingdom (2.8%), and from France (2.3%).

The 2010s

The exports of China were $2.3 trillion per year in the 2010s, ranked 1st in the world, and were on a par with the USA ($2.3 trillion). The share in the world was 10.1%, and 26.5% from Asia.

The structure of exports: primary products (3.2%), resource-based manufactures (8.3%), low technology manufactures (30.9%), medium technology manufactures (24.3%), and high technology manufactures (32.9%).

China exported goods to the USA (17.9%), Hong Kong (14.4%), Japan (6.6%), Republic of Korea (4.4%), Germany (3.3%) and other countries (53.5%).

The share of exports in GDP of China was 21.8% in the 2010s, ranked 167th in the world, and was on a par with Eastern Africa (21.9%), Uzbekistan (21.7%).

The exports per capita from China were $1 635.3 in the 2010s, ranked 123rd in the world, and were on a par with Melanesia ($1 626.0), the Dominican Republic ($1 645.9), Jamaica ($1 654.0). The China's exports per capita were less than exports per capita in the world ($3 098.9) by 47.2%, and were less than exports per capita from Asia ($1 964.3) by 16.7%.

The growth of exports from China was 6.8% in the 2010s, ranked 44th in the world, and was on a par with Turkey (6.8%), Saint Kitts and Nevis (6.8%). The growth of exports from China (6.8%) was greater than growth of exports in the world (4.4%), was greater than growth of exports from Asia (5.3%).

Comparison with neighbors. The exports of China were 2.7 times higher than from Japan ($859.4 billion), 3.5 times higher than from South Korea ($658.6 billion), 4.7 times higher than from Russia ($488.7 billion), 4.9 times higher than from India ($467.2 billion), 13.1 times higher than from Vietnam ($175.2 billion), 32.4 times higher than from Kazakhstan ($70.9 billion), and 156.9 times higher than from Myanmar ($14.6 billion). The value of exports per capita from China was 4.6 times higher than from India ($358.9) and 5.9 times higher than from Myanmar ($278.9); but 8.0 times lower than from Republic of Korea ($13.0 thousand), 4.1 times lower than from Japan ($6.7 thousand), 2.5 times lower than from Kazakhstan ($4.1 thousand), 2.1 times lower than from Russia ($3.4 thousand), and 13.9% lower than from Vietnam ($1 900.3). The growth of exports from China was greater than from India (5.8%), from Republic of Korea (5.0%), from Japan (4.6%), from Russia (2.9%), and from Kazakhstan (1.9%); but less than from Vietnam (13.4%) and from Myanmar (9.0%).

Comparison with leaders. The value of exports from China was 1.0% higher than from the USA ($2.3 trillion), 36.2% higher than from Germany ($1.7 trillion), 2.7 times higher than from Japan ($859.4 billion), 2.8 times higher than from the UK ($815.1 billion), and 2.9 times higher than from France ($802.0 billion). The value of exports per capita from China was 12.6 times lower than from Germany ($20.6 thousand), 7.6 times lower than from the UK ($12.4 thousand), 7.4 times lower than from France ($12.1 thousand), 4.3 times lower than from the USA ($7.1 thousand), and 4.1 times lower than from Japan ($6.7 thousand). The growth of exports from China was greater than from Germany (4.7%), from Japan (4.6%), from France (4.0%), from the USA (3.7%), and from the United Kingdom (3.1%).

Chapter XI. Imports

Imports of goods and services

The Chinese imports increased from $7.8 billion per year in the 1970s to $2.1 trillion per year in the 2010s, that is by $2.1 trillion or 264.4 times. The change occurred at $843.1 billion due to a 1.7-fold increase in prices, as also at $1.2 trillion due to a 102.1-fold increase in per capita rate, as well as at $4.2 billion due to the increase in population. The average annual growth in imports is 13.1%. The minimum value of imports was in 1970 at $2.6 billion. The maximum value of imports was in 2018 at $2.5 trillion.

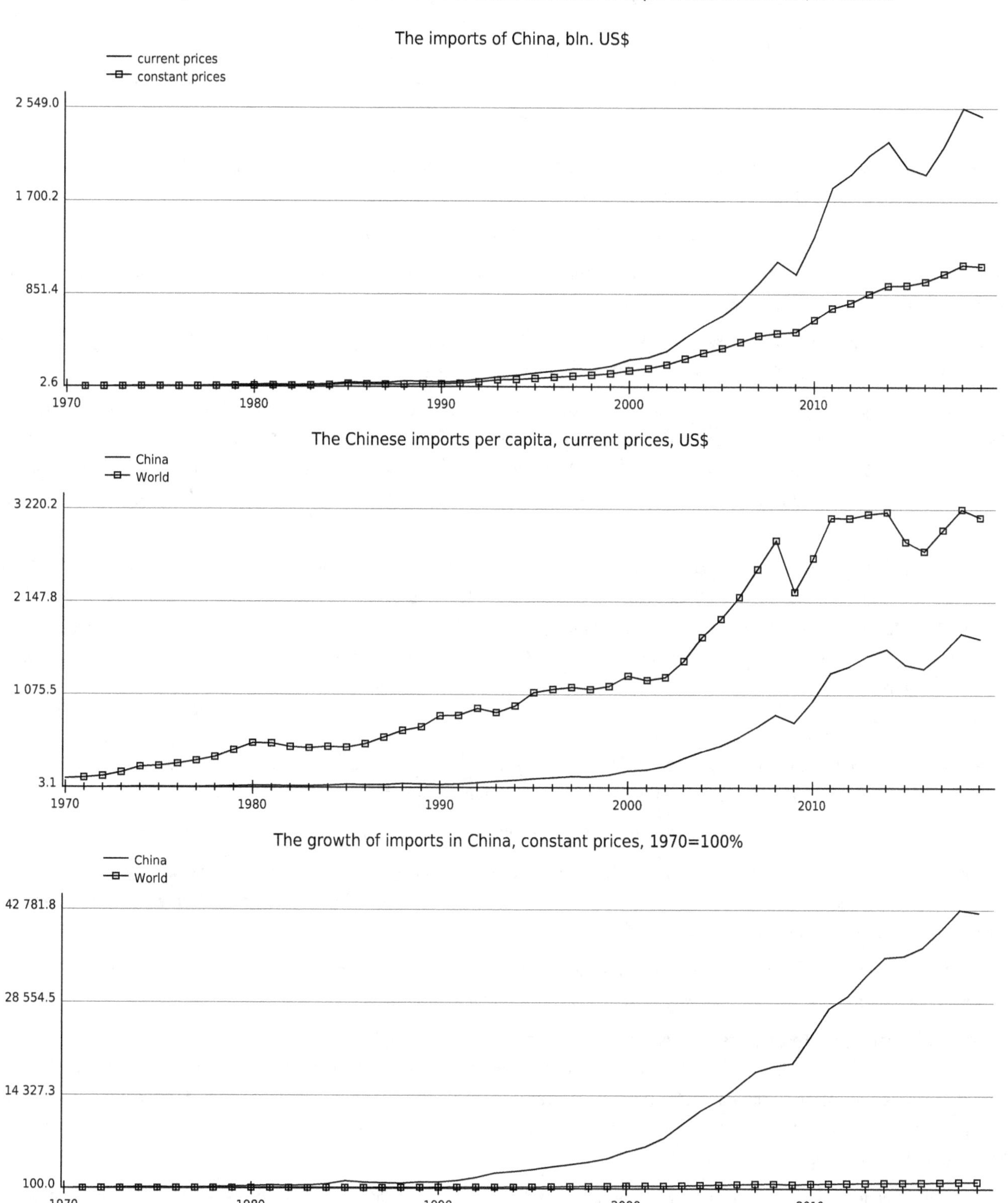

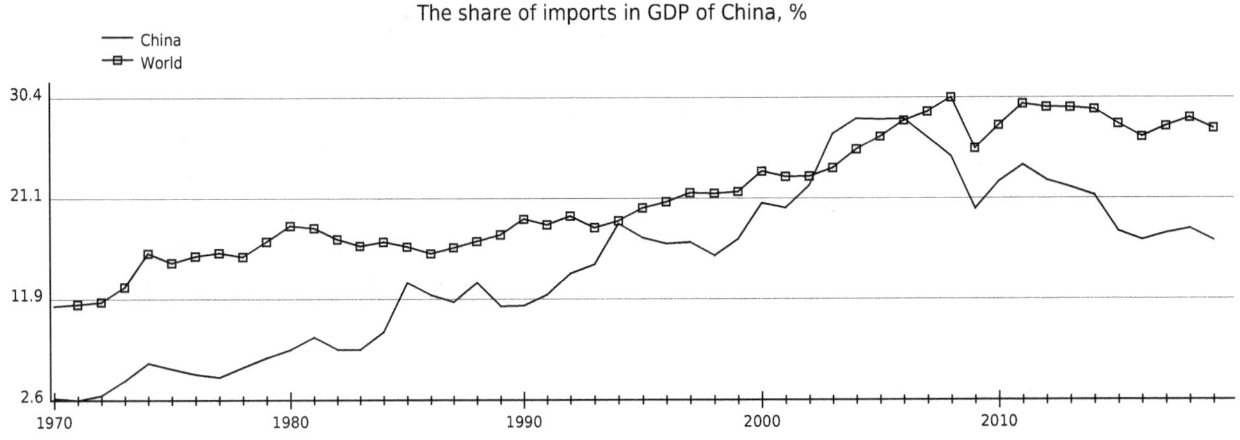

The 1970s

The China's imports were $7.8 billion per year in the 1970s, ranked 28th in the world, and were on a par with Republic of Korea ($7.9 billion), Eastern Africa ($7.9 billion), Venezuela ($8.0 billion). The share in the world was 0.79%, and 4.2% in Asia.

The share of imports in GDP of China was 5.0% in the 1970s, ranked 183rd in the world.

The China's imports per capita were $8.6 in the 1970s, ranked 182nd in the world. The value of imports per capita in China was less than imports per capita in the world ($244.3) in 28.5 times, and was less than imports per capita in Asia ($79.6) in 9.3 times.

The growth of imports in China was 16.5% in the 1970s, ranked 10th in the world. The growth of imports in China (16.5%) was greater than growth of imports in the world (6.3%), was greater than growth of imports in Asia (9.6%).

Comparison with neighbors. The imports of China were greater than in India ($6.0 billion), in Vietnam ($1.6 billion), and in Myanmar ($353.3 million); but less than in Japan ($61.0 billion) and in Republic of Korea ($7.9 billion). The Chinese imports per capita were less than in Japan ($547.6), in Republic of Korea ($225.2), in Vietnam ($33.0), in Myanmar ($11.7), and in India ($9.7). The growth of imports in China was greater than in Japan (7.0%), in India (6.2%), in Vietnam (4.7%), and in Myanmar (3.2%); but less than in South Korea (18.3%).

Comparison with leaders. The value of imports in China was less than in the USA ($133.2 billion), in Germany ($92.5 billion), in France ($63.3 billion), in the United Kingdom ($62.4 billion), and in Japan ($61.0 billion). The imports per capita in China were less than in France ($1 181.1), in Germany ($1 175.1), in the United Kingdom ($1 113.2), in the United States ($610.4), and in Japan ($547.6). The growth of imports in China was greater than in France (7.2%), in Japan (7.0%), in Germany (5.6%), in the United States (5.1%), and in the UK (4.5%).

The 1980s

The Chinese imports were $34.0 billion per year in the 1980s, ranked 17th in the world, and were on a par with Singapore ($33.4 billion), South Korea ($34.7 billion). The share in the world was 1.3%, and 5.6% in Asia.

The share of imports in GDP of China was 10.3% in the 1980s, ranked 174th in the world.

The value of imports per capita in China was $31.7 in the 1980s, ranked 176th in the world, and was on a par with Bangladesh ($30.9). The value of imports per capita in China was less than imports per capita in the world ($539.1) in 17.0 times, and was less than imports per capita in Asia ($211.9) in 6.7 times.

The growth of imports in China was 10.5% in the 1980s, ranked 9th in the world. The growth of imports in China (10.5%) was greater than growth of imports in the world (3.8%), was greater than growth of imports in Asia (4.9%).

Comparison with neighbors. The imports of China were greater than in India ($18.8 billion), in Vietnam ($1.5 billion), and in Myanmar ($509.0 million); but less than in Japan ($175.9 billion) and in Republic of Korea ($34.7 billion). The China's imports per capita were greater than in Vietnam ($25.3), in India ($24.3), and in Myanmar ($13.5); but less than in Japan ($1 450.4) and in South Korea ($859.4). The growth of imports in China was greater than in Republic of Korea (8.8%), in India (7.1%), in Japan (4.6%), in Vietnam (3.8%), and in Myanmar (-3.2%).

Comparison with leaders. The China's imports were less than in the USA ($417.2 billion), in Germany ($225.6 billion), in Japan ($175.9

billion), in France ($162.0 billion), and in the UK ($157.7 billion). The value of imports per capita in China was less than in Germany ($2.9 thousand), in France ($2.9 thousand), in the UK ($2.8 thousand), in the USA ($1 742.4), and in Japan ($1 450.4). The growth of imports in China was greater than in the USA (5.8%), in the UK (5.1%), in Japan (4.6%), in France (4.3%), and in Germany (3.3%).

The 1990s

The value of imports in China was $115.9 billion per year in the 1990s, ranked 13th in the world, and was on a par with Switzerland ($114.9 billion), Republic of Korea ($118.6 billion), Central America ($118.8 billion). The share in the world was 2.0%, and 7.8% in Asia.

The share of imports in GDP of China was 16.2% in the 1990s, ranked 195th in the world, and was on a par with Bangladesh (16.1%).

The Chinese imports per capita were $94.0 in the 1990s, ranked 184th in the world, and were on a par with Cambodia ($94.0), Mali ($93.7), Mozambique ($95.1). The Chinese imports per capita were less than imports per capita in the world ($1 015.5) in 10.8 times, and were less than imports per capita in Asia ($430.1) in 4.6 times.

The growth of imports in China was 16% in the 1990s, ranked 7th in the world. The growth of imports in China (16.0%) was greater than growth of imports in the world (6.6%), was greater than growth of imports in Asia (6.8%).

Comparison with neighbors. The value of imports in China was greater than in Russia ($108.7 billion), in India ($39.9 billion), in Kazakhstan ($10.6 billion), in Vietnam ($8.5 billion), and in Myanmar ($2.4 billion); but less than in Japan ($355.9 billion) and in South Korea ($118.6 billion). The imports per capita in China were greater than in Myanmar ($54.0) and in India ($41.8); but less than in Japan ($2.8 thousand), in South Korea ($2.6 thousand), in Russia ($735.2), in Kazakhstan ($669.7), and in Vietnam ($115.4). The growth of imports in China was greater than in Vietnam (15.4%), in India (12.9%), in South Korea (9.8%), in Myanmar (5.2%), in Japan (3.3%), in Russia (2.9%), and in Kazakhstan (-14.0%).

Comparison with leaders. The Chinese imports were less than in the United States ($874.1 billion), in Germany ($501.6 billion), in Japan ($355.9 billion), in the UK ($330.2 billion), and in France ($308.5 billion). The imports per capita in China were less than in Germany ($6.2 thousand), in the UK ($5.7 thousand), in France ($5.2 thousand), in the United States ($3.3 thousand), and in Japan ($2.8 thousand). The growth of imports in China was greater than in the USA (8.3%), in Germany (6.4%), in France (5.1%), in the UK (5.1%), and in Japan (3.3%).

The 2000s

The China's imports were $641.1 billion per year in the 2000s, ranked 4th in the world, and were on a par with the UK ($641.8 billion). The share in the world was 5.2%, and 18.1% in Asia.

The structure of imports: primary products (16.0%), resource-based manufactures (15.9%), low technology manufactures (7.7%), medium technology manufactures (26.5%), and high technology manufactures (33.3%).

China imported goods from Hong Kong (21.3%), Japan (13.1%), Republic of Korea (9.4%), the USA (7.4%), Taiwan (6.1%) and other countries (42.6%).

The share of imports in GDP of China was 24.7% in the 2000s, ranked 185th in the world, and was on a par with Uzbekistan (24.8%), Turkey (24.9%).

The Chinese imports per capita were $483.3 in the 2000s, ranked 158th in the world. The China's imports per capita were less than imports per capita in the world ($1 899.9) in 3.9 times, and were less than imports per capita in Asia ($898.2) by 46.2%.

The growth of imports in China was 15.1% in the 2000s, ranked 8th in the world. The growth of imports in China (15.1%) was greater than growth of imports in the world (5.1%), was greater than growth of imports in Asia (7.8%).

Comparison with neighbors. The imports of China were greater than in Japan ($566.4 billion), in South Korea ($299.8 billion), in India ($186.2 billion), in Russia ($172.4 billion), in Vietnam ($43.2 billion), in Kazakhstan ($25.5 billion), and in Myanmar ($3.1 billion). The Chinese imports per capita were greater than in India ($163.6) and in Myanmar ($64.3); but less than in South Korea ($6.2 thousand), in Japan ($4.4 thousand), in Kazakhstan ($1 659.2), in Russia ($1 194.9), and in Vietnam ($517.1). The growth of imports in China was greater than in Russia (14.0%), in India (13.5%), in Vietnam (12.3%), in Republic of Korea (8.1%), in Kazakhstan (5.1%), in Myanmar (2.6%), and in Japan (1.8%).

Comparison with leaders. The imports of China were greater than in Japan ($566.4 billion) and in France ($566.1 billion); but less than in the USA ($1.9 trillion), in Germany ($914.7 billion), and in the United Kingdom ($641.8 billion). The Chinese imports per capita were less than in Germany ($11.2 thousand), in the United Kingdom ($10.6 thousand), in France ($9.0 thousand), in the USA ($6.4 thousand), and in Japan ($4.4 thousand). The growth of imports in China was greater than in Germany (3.7%), in France (3.5%), in the United Kingdom (3.1%), in the United States (2.8%), and in Japan (1.8%).

The 2010s

The imports of China were $2.1 trillion per year in the 2010s, ranked 2nd in the world. The share in the world was 9.4%, and 25.9% in Asia.

The structure of imports: primary products (21.2%), resource-based manufactures (18.4%), low technology manufactures (4.7%), medium technology manufactures (22.0%), and high technology manufactures (29.6%).

China imported goods from Hong Kong (17.8%), Republic of Korea (8.7%), Japan (8.5%), the United States (7.2%), Germany (5.7%) and other countries (52.1%).

The share of imports in GDP of China was 19.7% in the 2010s, ranked 200th in the world, and was on a par with Iran (19.6%).

The value of imports per capita in China was $1 475.4 in the 2010s, ranked 140th in the world, and was on a par with Algeria ($1 467.8), Morocco ($1 447.0). The imports per capita in China were less than imports per capita in the world ($3 015.6) in 2.0 times, and were less than imports per capita in Asia ($1 813.7) by 18.7%.

The growth of imports in China was 8.2% in the 2010s, ranked 27th in the world. The growth of imports in China (8.2%) was greater than growth of imports in the world (4.4%), was greater than growth of imports in Asia (5.4%).

Comparison with neighbors. The imports of China were 2.4 times higher than in Japan ($877.9 billion), 3.5 times higher than in South Korea ($596.5 billion), 3.8 times higher than in India ($546.0 billion), 5.7 times higher than in Russia ($364.2 billion), 12.0 times higher than in Vietnam ($172.2 billion), 41.5 times higher than in Kazakhstan ($49.9 billion), and 116.3 times higher than in Myanmar ($17.8 billion). The Chinese imports per capita were 3.5 times higher than in India ($419.4) and 4.3 times higher than in Myanmar ($339.4); but 8.0 times lower than in Republic of Korea ($11.8 thousand), 4.7 times lower than in Japan ($6.9 thousand), 48.5% lower than in Kazakhstan ($2.9 thousand), 41.4% lower than in Russia ($2.5 thousand), and 21.0% lower than in Vietnam ($1 868.0). The growth of imports in China was greater than in South Korea (5.3%), in Kazakhstan (4.9%), in India (4.6%), in Japan (3.8%), and in Russia (3.5%); but less than in Vietnam (12.8%) and in Myanmar (10.5%).

Comparison with leaders. The Chinese imports were 42.2% higher than in Germany ($1.5 trillion), 2.4 times higher than in Japan ($877.9 billion), 2.4 times higher than in the United Kingdom ($854.8 billion), and 2.5 times higher than in France ($831.9 billion); but 26.6% lower than in the United States ($2.8 trillion). The Chinese imports per capita were 12.0 times lower than in Germany ($17.8 thousand), 8.8 times lower than in the United Kingdom ($13.0 thousand), 8.5 times lower than in France ($12.5 thousand), 6.0 times lower than in the USA ($8.8 thousand), and 4.7 times lower than in Japan ($6.9 thousand). The growth of imports in China was greater than in Germany (4.8%), in the USA (4.4%), in France (4.1%), in Japan (3.8%), and in the United Kingdom (3.6%).

Part IV. Consumption

Chapter XII. Government consumption expenditure

General government final consumption expenditure

The government expenditure of China grew from $19.4 billion per year in the 1970s to $1.7 trillion per year in the 2010s, that is by $1.7 trillion or 86.7 times. The change occurred at $879.9 billion due to a 2.1-fold increase in prices, as also at $769.4 billion due to a 26.9-fold increase in per capita rate, as well as at $10.3 billion due to the expansion in population. The average annual growth in government consumption expenditure is 9.4%. The minimum value of government expenditure was in 1970 at $10.1 billion. The maximum value of government expenditure was in 2019 at $2.4 trillion.

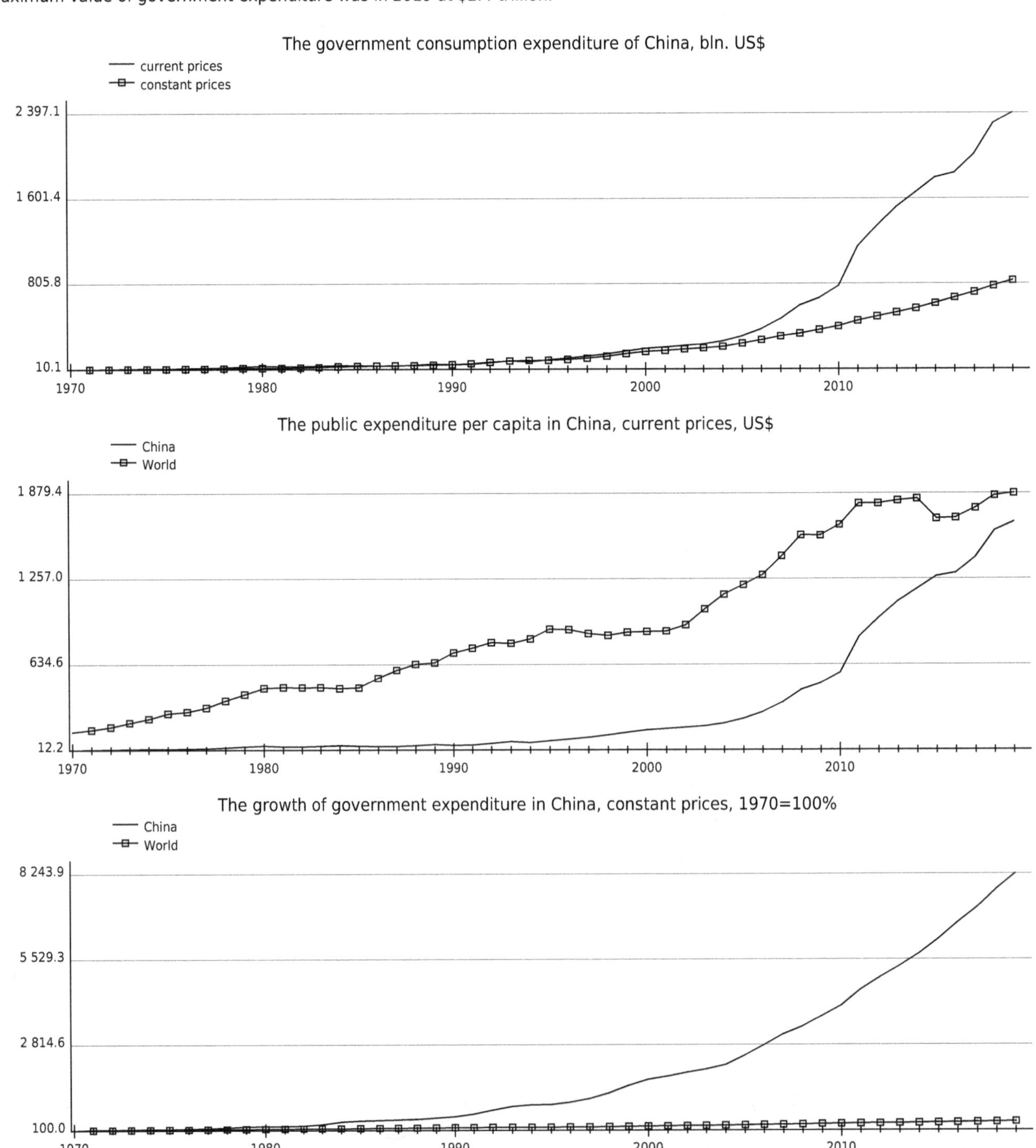

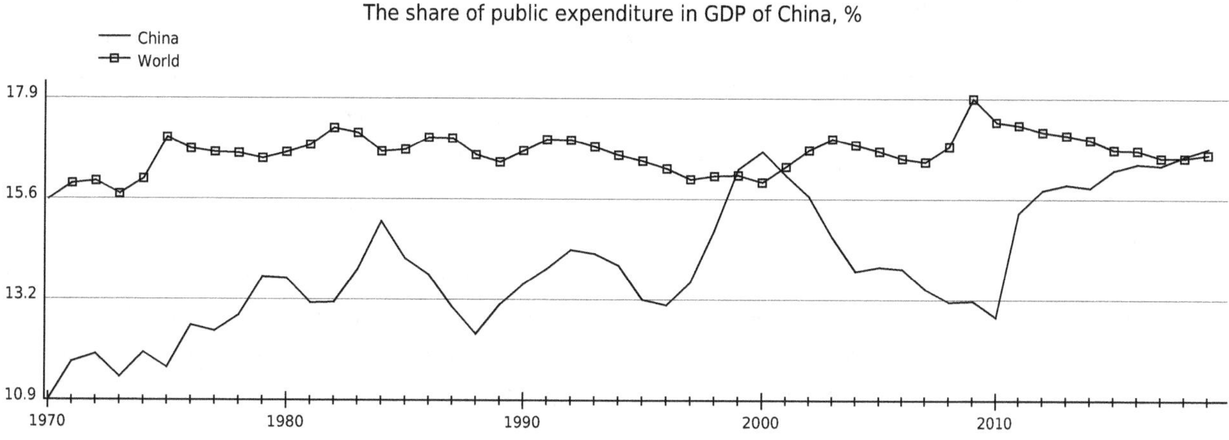

The 1970s

The public expenditure of China was $19.4 billion per year in the 1970s, ranked 10th in the world, and was on a par with Oceania ($19.6 billion). The share in the world was 1.8%, and 12.1% in Asia.

The share of public expenditure in GDP of China was 12.4% in the 1970s, ranked 129th in the world, and was on a par with Barbados (12.4%), Honduras (12.5%), Belize (12.5%).

The China's public expenditure per capita was $21.2 in the 1970s, ranked 168th in the world. The public expenditure per capita in China was less than public expenditure per capita in the world ($265.2) in 12.5 times, and was less than government expenditure per capita in Asia ($68.9) in 3.3 times.

The growth of public expenditure in China was 9.3% in the 1970s, ranked 32nd in the world, and was on a par with Ivory Coast (9.3%), the Seychelles (9.3%). The growth of government consumption expenditure in China (9.3%) was greater than growth of government expenditure in the world (3.7%), was greater than growth of government expenditure in Asia (6.9%).

Comparison with neighbors. The China's government consumption expenditure was greater than in India ($9.3 billion), in Republic of Korea ($2.8 billion), in Myanmar ($498.8 million), and in Vietnam ($292.6 million); but less than in the USSR ($117.3 billion) and in Japan ($78.0 billion). The government consumption expenditure per capita in China was greater than in Myanmar ($16.5), in India ($15.1), and in Vietnam ($6.1); but less than in Japan ($700.2), in the USSR ($465.0), and in South Korea ($79.0). The growth of government consumption expenditure in China was greater than in the USSR (7.2%), in Republic of Korea (5.8%), in Japan (5.3%), in Vietnam (4.7%), in India (4.5%), and in Myanmar (3.1%).

Comparison with leaders. The public expenditure of China was less than in the USA ($285.9 billion), in the USSR ($117.3 billion), in Germany ($95.6 billion), in Japan ($78.0 billion), and in France ($64.5 billion). The Chinese government expenditure per capita was less than in the United States ($1 310.2), in Germany ($1 213.7), in France ($1 202.3), in Japan ($700.2), and in the USSR ($465.0). The growth of government consumption expenditure in China was greater than in the USSR (7.2%), in Japan (5.3%), in France (5.0%), in Germany (4.4%), and in the United States (0.94%).

The 1980s

The Chinese government consumption expenditure was $44.6 billion per year in the 1980s, ranked 9th in the world, and was on a par with Australasia ($44.9 billion), the Netherlands ($43.7 billion). The share in the world was 1.8%, and 9.2% in Asia.

The share of government consumption expenditure in GDP of China was 13.5% in the 1980s, ranked 125th in the world, and was on a par with the Maldives (13.5%), Portugal (13.4%), Mauritius (13.4%).

The government consumption expenditure per capita in China was $41.6 in the 1980s, ranked 164th in the world, and was on a par with Uganda ($41.5), Pakistan ($41.9), Haiti ($40.7). The China's government consumption expenditure per capita was less than government consumption expenditure per capita in the world ($523.5) in 12.6 times, and was less than public expenditure per capita in Asia ($170.1) in 4.1 times.

The growth of public expenditure in China was 8.2% in the 1980s, ranked 16th in the world. The growth of government expenditure in China (8.2%) was greater than growth of public expenditure in the world (2.7%), was greater than growth of public expenditure in Asia (4.2%).

Comparison with neighbors. The government consumption expenditure of China was greater than in India ($26.2 billion), in South Korea ($13.0 billion), in Myanmar ($746.3 million), and in Vietnam ($286.0 million); but less than in Japan ($257.4 billion) and in the USSR ($181.1 billion). The public expenditure per capita in China was greater than in India ($33.8), in Myanmar ($19.9), and in Vietnam ($4.7); but less than in Japan ($2.1 thousand), in the USSR ($658.0), and in Republic of Korea ($321.0). The growth of government expenditure in China was greater than in India (6.9%), in South Korea (6.5%), in the USSR (5.4%), in Vietnam (5.0%), in Japan (3.5%), and in Myanmar (1.5%).

Comparison with leaders. The China's government expenditure was less than in the USA ($665.3 billion), in Japan ($257.4 billion), in Germany ($203.7 billion), in the USSR ($181.1 billion), and in France ($159.8 billion). The public expenditure per capita in China was less than in France ($2.8 thousand), in the United States ($2.8 thousand), in Germany ($2.6 thousand), in Japan ($2.1 thousand), and in the USSR ($658.0). The growth of government consumption expenditure in China was greater than in the USSR (5.4%), in Japan (3.5%), in France (2.8%), in the United States (2.6%), and in Germany (0.98%).

The 1990s

The public expenditure of China was $102.2 billion per year in the 1990s, ranked 9th in the world, and was on a par with Spain ($102.0 billion). The share in the world was 2.2%, and 9.3% in Asia.

The share of public expenditure in GDP of China was 14.3% in the 1990s, ranked 124th in the world, and was on a par with Asia (14.2%), Aruba (14.4%), Cyprus (14.1%).

The China's government expenditure per capita was $82.9 in the 1990s, ranked 165th in the world, and was on a par with Kyrgyzstan ($83.1), Cameroon ($84.8). The government consumption expenditure per capita in China was less than public expenditure per capita in the world ($824.8) in 9.9 times, and was less than government expenditure per capita in Asia ($318.7) in 3.8 times.

The growth of government expenditure in China was 12% in the 1990s, ranked 5th in the world. The growth of government expenditure in China (12.0%) was greater than growth of government expenditure in the world (2.0%), was greater than growth of public expenditure in Asia (5.0%).

Comparison with neighbors. The China's public expenditure was greater than in Russia ($74.6 billion), in Republic of Korea ($47.3 billion), in India ($40.1 billion), in Kazakhstan ($2.9 billion), in Vietnam ($1.4 billion), and in Myanmar ($858.9 million); but less than in Japan ($651.8 billion). The government consumption expenditure per capita in China was greater than in India ($42.0), in Myanmar ($19.6), and in Vietnam ($18.8); but less than in Japan ($5.2 thousand), in South Korea ($1 050.9), in Russia ($504.2), and in Kazakhstan ($183.2). The growth of public expenditure in China was greater than in Vietnam (6.6%), in India (6.1%), in South Korea (5.1%), in Myanmar (3.5%), in Japan (3.0%), in Russia (-2.7%), and in Kazakhstan (-6.6%).

Comparison with leaders. The Chinese government consumption expenditure was less than in the United States ($1.1 trillion), in Japan ($651.8 billion), in Germany ($419.6 billion), in France ($325.4 billion), and in the United Kingdom ($234.6 billion). The China's government consumption expenditure per capita was less than in France ($5.5 thousand), in Germany ($5.2 thousand), in Japan ($5.2 thousand), in the United States ($4.3 thousand), and in the UK ($4.1 thousand). The growth of government expenditure in China was greater than in Japan (3.0%), in Germany (2.4%), in the UK (2.1%), in France (1.8%), and in the USA (1.3%).

The 2000s

The public expenditure of China was $362.5 billion per year in the 2000s, ranked 6th in the world. The share in the world was 4.6%, and 19.2% in Asia.

The share of government expenditure in GDP of China was 14.0% in the 2000s, ranked 124th in the world, and was on a par with Bermuda (14.0%), Uzbekistan (14.0%), Thailand (14.0%).

The China's government consumption expenditure per capita was $273.3 in the 2000s, ranked 139th in the world, and was on a par with Northern Africa ($273.2), Albania ($269.4). The China's government consumption expenditure per capita was less than government expenditure per capita in the world ($1 200.9) in 4.4 times, and was less than government consumption expenditure per capita in Asia ($477.4) by 42.8%.

The growth of public expenditure in China was 9.3% in the 2000s, ranked 21st in the world, and was on a par with the Turks and Caicos Islands (9.3%), Jordan (9.4%). The growth of government expenditure in China (9.3%) was greater than growth of public expenditure in the world (3.1%), was greater than growth of government expenditure in Asia (5.3%).

Comparison with neighbors. The Chinese government expenditure was greater than in Russia ($136.2 billion), in South Korea ($108.9 billion), in India ($89.0 billion), in Kazakhstan ($7.0 billion), in Vietnam ($3.4 billion), and in Myanmar ($1.4 billion); but less than in Japan ($844.2 billion). The government expenditure per capita in China was greater than in India ($78.2), in Vietnam ($41.1), and in Myanmar ($28.1); but less than in Japan ($6.6 thousand), in Republic of Korea ($2.2 thousand), in Russia ($943.7), and in Kazakhstan ($454.3). The growth of public expenditure in China was greater than in Kazakhstan (7.9%), in Vietnam (7.2%), in India (5.7%), in South Korea (5.4%), in Russia (1.7%), and in Japan (1.7%); but less than in Myanmar (10.7%).

Comparison with leaders. The China's government expenditure was less than in the United States ($1.9 trillion), in Japan ($844.2 billion), in Germany ($520.1 billion), in France ($479.9 billion), and in the United Kingdom ($453.4 billion). The government consumption expenditure per capita in China was less than in France ($7.6 thousand), in the UK ($7.5 thousand), in Japan ($6.6 thousand), in the USA ($6.5 thousand), and in Germany ($6.4 thousand). The growth of government consumption expenditure in China was greater than in the UK (2.9%), in the United States (2.2%), in Japan (1.7%), in France (1.7%), and in Germany (1.4%).

The 2010s

The Chinese public expenditure was $1.7 trillion per year in the 2010s, ranked 2nd in the world. The share in the world was 12.8%, and 39.2% in Asia.

The share of government expenditure in GDP of China was 16.0% in the 2010s, ranked 112th in the world, and was on a par with Bolivia (16.0%), El Salvador (16.0%), Belize (16.1%).

The government consumption expenditure per capita in China was $1 197.3 in the 2010s, ranked 101st in the world, and was on a par with Mexico ($1 173.5), Grenada ($1 221.5). The government consumption expenditure per capita in China was less than public expenditure per capita in the world ($1 785.1) by 32.9%, and was greater than public expenditure per capita in Asia ($970.7) by 23.3%.

The growth of government expenditure in China was 8.3% in the 2010s, ranked 15th in the world. The growth of government expenditure in China (8.3%) was greater than growth of government consumption expenditure in the world (2.3%), was greater than growth of government expenditure in Asia (5.2%).

Comparison with neighbors. The government expenditure of China was 61.0% higher than in Japan ($1.0 trillion), 5.2 times higher than in Russia ($320.0 billion), 7.1 times higher than in India ($236.7 billion), 7.6 times higher than in Republic of Korea ($222.1 billion), 86.4 times higher than in Kazakhstan ($19.4 billion), 140.7 times higher than in Vietnam ($11.9 billion), and 177.4 times higher than in Myanmar ($9.5 billion). The Chinese public expenditure per capita was 7.3% higher than in Kazakhstan ($1 116.1), 6.6 times higher than in India ($181.8), 6.6 times higher than in Myanmar ($180.6), and 9.2 times higher than in Vietnam ($129.4); but 6.8 times lower than in Japan ($8.2 thousand), 3.7 times lower than in South Korea ($4.4 thousand), and 45.8% lower than in Russia ($2.2 thousand). The growth of public expenditure in China was greater than in Vietnam (7.5%), in Myanmar (5.8%), in India (5.7%), in Republic of Korea (4.6%), in Kazakhstan (4.5%), in Japan (1.3%), and in Russia (0.51%).

Comparison with leaders. The Chinese government expenditure was 61.0% higher than in Japan ($1.0 trillion), 2.3 times higher than in Germany ($721.6 billion), 2.6 times higher than in France ($637.9 billion), and 3.1 times higher than in the United Kingdom ($548.8 billion); but 36.7% lower than in the United States ($2.7 trillion). The China's government consumption expenditure per capita was 8.0 times lower than in France ($9.6 thousand), 7.4 times lower than in Germany ($8.8 thousand), 7.0 times lower than in the UK ($8.4 thousand), 6.9 times lower than in the United States ($8.3 thousand), and 6.8 times lower than in Japan ($8.2 thousand). The growth of government expenditure in China was greater than in Germany (1.9%), in Japan (1.3%), in France (1.3%), in the UK (1.2%), and in the United States (0.0052%).

Chapter XIII. Household consumption expenditure

(including Non-profit institutions serving households)

The China's household expenditure grew up from $79.3 billion per year in the 1970s to $3.9 trillion per year in the 2010s, that is by $3.9 trillion or 49.5 times. The change occurred at $2.0 trillion due to a 2.0-fold increase in prices, as also at $1.8 trillion due to a 15.9-fold increase in per capita rate, as well as at $42.4 billion due to the rise in population. The average annual growth in household consumption expenditure is 7.9%. The minimum value of household consumption expenditure was in 1970 at $49.0 billion. The maximum value of household consumption expenditure was in 2019 at $5.6 trillion.

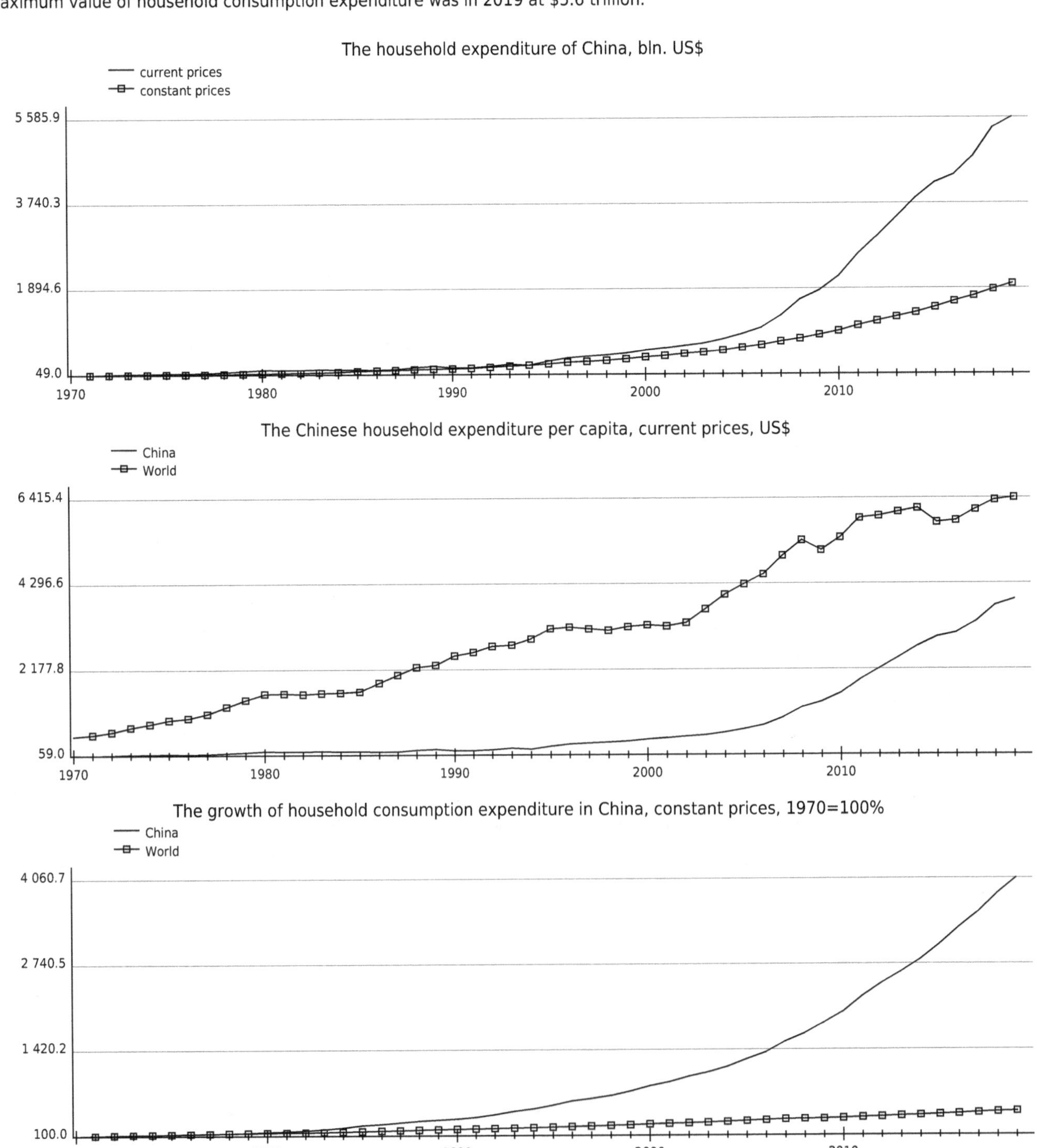

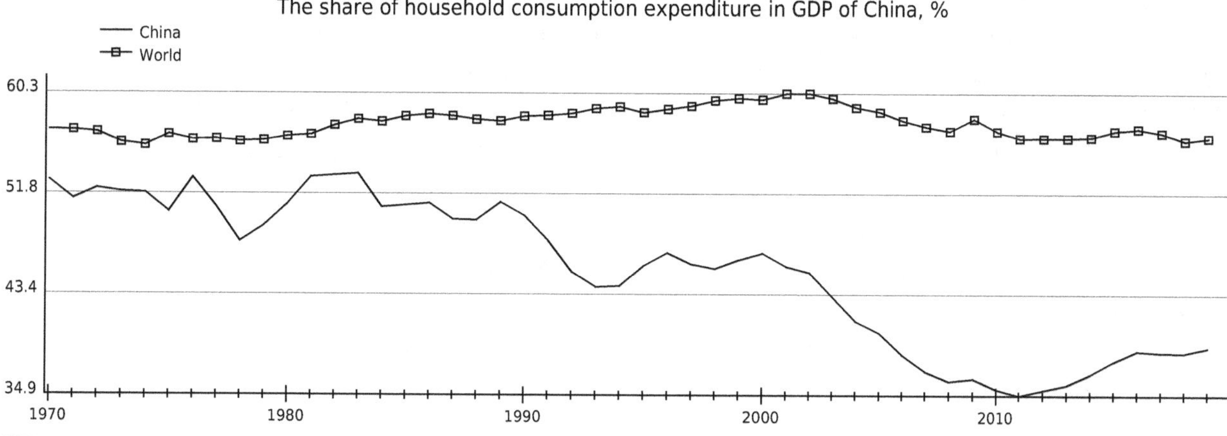

The 1970s

The household expenditure of China was $79.3 billion per year in the 1970s, ranked 9th in the world, and was on a par with India ($77.8 billion), Western Asia ($77.4 billion). The share in the world was 2.1%, and 12.1% in Asia.

The share of household consumption expenditure in GDP of China was 50.7% in the 1970s, ranked 152nd in the world, and was on a par with Romania (50.7%), Israel (50.8%), Eastern Asia (50.6%).

The household consumption expenditure per capita in China was $86.8 in the 1970s, ranked 181st in the world, and was on a par with Iraq ($88.8). The China's household expenditure per capita was less than household consumption expenditure per capita in the world ($914.8) in 10.5 times, and was less than household consumption expenditure per capita in Asia ($282.4) in 3.3 times.

The growth of household expenditure in China was 4.3% in the 1970s, ranked 85th in the world, and was on a par with Portugal (4.3%), Congo (4.3%), Suriname (4.4%). The growth of household consumption expenditure in China (4.3%) was greater than growth of household consumption expenditure in the world (4.1%), was less than growth of household expenditure in Asia (5.2%).

Comparison with neighbors. The household consumption expenditure of China was greater than in India ($77.8 billion), in Republic of Korea ($17.4 billion), in Vietnam ($3.9 billion), and in Myanmar ($3.0 billion); but less than in the USSR ($310.6 billion) and in Japan ($280.9 billion). The household expenditure per capita in China was greater than in Vietnam ($81.4); but less than in Japan ($2.5 thousand), in the USSR ($1 231.6), in Republic of Korea ($497.5), in India ($126.1), and in Myanmar ($99.2). The growth of household expenditure in China was greater than in Myanmar (3.1%) and in India (2.7%); but less than in Republic of Korea (7.6%), in Japan (5.1%), in the USSR (4.7%), and in Vietnam (4.7%).

Comparison with leaders. The China's household expenditure was less than in the United States ($1.0 trillion), in the USSR ($310.6 billion), in Japan ($280.9 billion), in Germany ($277.8 billion), and in France ($180.7 billion). The China's household expenditure per capita was less than in the USA ($4.7 thousand), in Germany ($3.5 thousand), in France ($3.4 thousand), in Japan ($2.5 thousand), and in the USSR ($1 231.6). The growth of household expenditure in China was greater than in France (4.0%), in the USA (3.6%), and in Germany (3.6%); but less than in Japan (5.1%) and in the USSR (4.7%).

The 1980s

The household consumption expenditure of China was $169.3 billion per year in the 1980s, ranked 10th in the world. The share in the world was 1.9%, and 9.0% in Asia.

The share of household expenditure in GDP of China was 51.3% in the 1980s, ranked 152nd in the world, and was on a par with French Polynesia (51.2%), Luxembourg (51.2%), Finland (51.6%).

The China's household consumption expenditure per capita was $157.8 in the 1980s, ranked 177th in the world, and was on a par with Ethiopia ($157.3). The household consumption expenditure per capita in China was less than household consumption expenditure per capita in the world ($1 808.0) in 11.5 times, and was less than household expenditure per capita in Asia ($666.0) in 4.2 times.

The growth of household expenditure in China was 8.8% in the 1980s, ranked 6th in the world. The growth of household expenditure in China (8.8%) was greater than growth of household consumption expenditure in the world (3.0%), was greater than growth of household consumption expenditure in Asia (4.7%).

Comparison with neighbors. The Chinese household expenditure was greater than in South Korea ($65.8 billion), in Myanmar ($4.6 billion), and in Vietnam ($3.8 billion); but less than in Japan ($945.6 billion), in the USSR ($424.6 billion), and in India ($176.1 billion). The Chinese household expenditure per capita was greater than in Myanmar ($121.2) and in Vietnam ($62.7); but less than in Japan ($7.8 thousand), in Republic of Korea ($1 627.9), in the USSR ($1 542.8), and in India ($226.8). The growth of household expenditure in China was greater than in South Korea (7.5%), in India (4.7%), in Vietnam (4.6%), in Japan (3.7%), in the USSR (3.0%), and in Myanmar (1.5%).

Comparison with leaders. The household expenditure of China was less than in the USA ($2.6 trillion), in Japan ($945.6 billion), in Germany ($575.7 billion), in the USSR ($424.6 billion), and in the UK ($416.5 billion). The China's household consumption expenditure per capita was less than in the United States ($10.9 thousand), in Japan ($7.8 thousand), in Germany ($7.4 thousand), in the United Kingdom ($7.4 thousand), and in the USSR ($1 542.8). The growth of household expenditure in China was greater than in Japan (3.7%), in the United Kingdom (3.5%), in the United States (3.2%), in the USSR (3.0%), and in Germany (1.8%).

The 1990s

The household consumption expenditure of China was $329.8 billion per year in the 1990s, ranked 10th in the world. The share in the world was 2.0%, and 7.9% in Asia.

The share of household expenditure in GDP of China was 46.0% in the 1990s, ranked 189th in the world, and was on a par with the Cook Islands (45.9%), Greenland (45.6%).

The household expenditure per capita in China was $267.5 in the 1990s, ranked 180th in the world, and was on a par with the CAR ($273.6), Laos ($273.9). The China's household expenditure per capita was less than household expenditure per capita in the world ($2 963.9) in 11.1 times, and was less than household consumption expenditure per capita in Asia ($1 208.2) in 4.5 times.

The growth of household consumption expenditure in China was 8.6% in the 1990s, ranked 7th in the world. The growth of household consumption expenditure in China (8.6%) was greater than growth of household consumption expenditure in the world (3.0%), was greater than growth of household expenditure in Asia (4.4%).

Comparison with neighbors. The household consumption expenditure of China was greater than in India ($234.2 billion), in Republic of Korea ($230.9 billion), in Russia ($198.5 billion), in Kazakhstan ($16.2 billion), in Vietnam ($13.4 billion), and in Myanmar ($6.1 billion); but less than in Japan ($2.3 trillion). The China's household expenditure per capita was greater than in India ($245.2), in Vietnam ($181.0), and in Myanmar ($139.1); but less than in Japan ($18.2 thousand), in South Korea ($5.1 thousand), in Russia ($1 342.0), and in Kazakhstan ($1 023.0). The growth of household expenditure in China was greater than in South Korea (6.3%), in India (4.8%), in Vietnam (4.8%), in Myanmar (3.5%), in Japan (1.8%), in Russia (-1.8%), and in Kazakhstan (-7.4%).

Comparison with leaders. The household consumption expenditure of China was less than in the United States ($4.9 trillion), in Japan ($2.3 trillion), in Germany ($1.2 trillion), in the UK ($884.5 billion), and in France ($783.0 billion). The Chinese household expenditure per capita was less than in the USA ($18.5 thousand), in Japan ($18.2 thousand), in the UK ($15.3 thousand), in Germany ($15.2 thousand), and in France ($13.2 thousand). The growth of household consumption expenditure in China was greater than in the United States (3.4%), in the United Kingdom (2.8%), in Germany (2.1%), in Japan (1.8%), and in France (1.8%).

The 2000s

The Chinese household expenditure was $1.0 trillion per year in the 2000s, ranked 7th in the world. The share in the world was 3.7%, and 15.6% in Asia.

The share of household consumption expenditure in GDP of China was 39.2% in the 2000s, ranked 193rd in the world, and was on a par with Bahrain (39.2%), Turkmenistan (39.3%).

The Chinese household consumption expenditure per capita was $766.3 in the 2000s, ranked 154th in the world, and was on a par with Mongolia ($765.7), Senegal ($753.1). The household expenditure per capita in China was less than household expenditure per capita in the world ($4 208.2) in 5.5 times, and was less than household expenditure per capita in Asia ($1 649.6) in 2.2 times.

The growth of household expenditure in China was 8.9% in the 2000s, ranked 14th in the world, and was on a par with Ethiopia (9.0%). The growth of household consumption expenditure in China (8.9%) was greater than growth of household expenditure in the world (3.0%), was greater than growth of household consumption expenditure in Asia (4.4%).

Comparison with neighbors. The China's household consumption expenditure was greater than in India ($483.5 billion), in South Korea

($445.9 billion), in Russia ($394.1 billion), in Vietnam ($40.1 billion), in Kazakhstan ($30.4 billion), and in Myanmar ($12.7 billion); but less than in Japan ($2.6 trillion). The household expenditure per capita in China was greater than in Vietnam ($480.4), in India ($424.8), and in Myanmar ($261.7); but less than in Japan ($20.4 thousand), in South Korea ($9.2 thousand), in Russia ($2.7 thousand), and in Kazakhstan ($1 979.9). The growth of household expenditure in China was greater than in Russia (8.6%), in Kazakhstan (7.9%), in Vietnam (6.2%), in India (5.2%), in South Korea (4.0%), and in Japan (0.81%); but less than in Myanmar (10.7%).

Comparison with leaders. The Chinese household consumption expenditure was less than in the United States ($8.5 trillion), in Japan ($2.6 trillion), in Germany ($1.5 trillion), in the United Kingdom ($1.5 trillion), and in France ($1.1 trillion). The household consumption expenditure per capita in China was less than in the USA ($28.8 thousand), in the United Kingdom ($25.0 thousand), in Japan ($20.4 thousand), in Germany ($18.9 thousand), and in France ($18.1 thousand). The growth of household expenditure in China was greater than in the United States (2.4%), in the United Kingdom (2.1%), in France (2.0%), in Japan (0.81%), and in Germany (0.46%).

The 2010s

The China's household expenditure was $3.9 trillion per year in the 2010s, ranked 2nd in the world. The share in the world was 8.9%, and 29.9% in Asia.

The share of household consumption expenditure in GDP of China was 37.4% in the 2010s, ranked 191st in the world, and was on a par with San Marino (37.4%), Algeria (37.7%).

The China's household expenditure per capita was $2 801.9 in the 2010s, ranked 129th in the world, and was on a par with Azerbaijan ($2.8 thousand), Suriname ($2.8 thousand), Micronesia ($2.8 thousand). The household consumption expenditure per capita in China was less than household expenditure per capita in the world ($6 018.5) in 2.1 times, and was less than household expenditure per capita in Asia ($2 977.2) by 5.9%.

The growth of household expenditure in China was 8.3% in the 2010s, ranked 10th in the world. The growth of household expenditure in China (8.3%) was greater than growth of household expenditure in the world (2.8%), was greater than growth of household consumption expenditure in Asia (4.9%).

Comparison with neighbors. The household consumption expenditure of China was 31.5% higher than in Japan ($3.0 trillion), 3.1 times higher than in India ($1.3 trillion), 4.3 times higher than in Russia ($914.4 billion), 5.5 times higher than in South Korea ($713.8 billion), 30.9 times higher than in Vietnam ($127.1 billion), 42.9 times higher than in Kazakhstan ($91.7 billion), and 106.4 times higher than in Myanmar ($36.9 billion). The China's household expenditure per capita was 2.0 times higher than in Vietnam ($1 378.2), 2.8 times higher than in India ($989.3), and 4.0 times higher than in Myanmar ($704.6); but 8.3 times lower than in Japan ($23.4 thousand), 5.0 times lower than in South Korea ($14.1 thousand), 2.3 times lower than in Russia ($6.3 thousand), and 46.8% lower than in Kazakhstan ($5.3 thousand). The growth of household consumption expenditure in China was greater than in India (6.8%), in Vietnam (6.7%), in Kazakhstan (6.1%), in Myanmar (6.0%), in Republic of Korea (2.5%), in Russia (2.4%), and in Japan (0.64%).

Comparison with leaders. The China's household consumption expenditure was 31.5% higher than in Japan ($3.0 trillion), 2.0 times higher than in Germany ($2.0 trillion), 2.2 times higher than in the United Kingdom ($1.8 trillion), and 2.7 times higher than in France ($1.5 trillion); but 3.1 times lower than in the USA ($12.2 trillion). The household expenditure per capita in China was 13.6 times lower than in the United States ($38.2 thousand), 9.7 times lower than in the United Kingdom ($27.2 thousand), 8.5 times lower than in Germany ($23.9 thousand), 8.3 times lower than in Japan ($23.4 thousand), and 7.9 times lower than in France ($22.0 thousand). The growth of household consumption expenditure in China was greater than in the United States (2.4%), in the UK (1.8%), in Germany (1.4%), in France (1.1%), and in Japan (0.64%).

Chapter XIV. Food consumption

During the research period the food consumption grew in alcoholic beverages (in 19.1 times), fruits (in 17.3 times), milk (in 15.3 times), treenuts (in 10.3 times), eggs (in 8.6 times), fish (in 7.5 times), vegetables (in 7.3 times), stimulants (in 6.2 times), meat (in 5.9 times), vegetable oils (in 3.9 times), sugar (in 2.2 times), spices (in 2.2 times), cereals (by 11.2%), but fell in starchy roots (by 59.0%), pulses (in 4.1 times).

These are the correlation coefficients between the GNI per capita in constant prices and the food consumption: treenuts (0.998), stimulants (0.996), milk (0.977), fruits (0.969), spices (0.942), alcoholic beverages (0.936), vegetables (0.921), fish (0.91), meat (0.903), eggs (0.856), vegetable oils (0.789), sugar (0.472), cereals (-0.129), starchy roots (-0.465), pulses (-0.656).

The 1970s

Kcal supply in China was 1 914.0 kcal/capita/day in the 1970s, ranked 133rd in the world, and was on a par with Vietnam (1 912.0 kcal/capita/day), Western Africa (1 909.8 kcal/capita/day), Yemen (1 923.4 kcal/capita/day). Kcal supply in China was less than in the world (2 403.2 kcal/capita/day), and was less than in Asia (2 080.9 kcal/capita/day). Structure of kcal supply: cereals (66.2%), starchy roots (15.1%), meat (4.6%), pulses (2.6%), vegetable oils (2.4%), and others (9.1%).

Protein supply in China was 47.5 g/capita/day in the 1970s, ranked 123rd in the world, and was on a par with Cape Verde (47.8 g/capita/day), Sierra Leone (47.1 g/capita/day). Protein supply in China was less than in the world (65.0 g/capita/day), and was less than in Asia (52.3 g/capita/day). Structure of protein supply: cereals (62%), starchy roots (6.9%), pulses (6.8%), meat (6.5%), vegetables (3.9%), and others (13.9%).

Fat supply in China was 25.4 g/capita/day in the 1970s, ranked 142nd in the world, and was on a par with Burkina Faso (25.5 g/capita/day). Fat supply in China was less than in the world (55.1 g/capita/day), and was less than in Asia (31.8 g/capita/day). Structure of fat supply: meat (32.7%), cereals (22.3%), vegetable oils (20.8%), starchy roots (3.2%), eggs (2.5%), and others (18.5%).

These are the levels of food consumption in the world rankings: 32nd - starchy roots (109.6 kg/capita/yr), 57th - cereals (135.8 kg/capita/yr), 63rd - vegetables (47.3 kg/capita/yr), 70th - pulses (5.3 kg/capita/yr), 80th - treenuts (0.24 kg/capita/yr), 86th - eggs (2.2 kg/capita/yr), 105th - spices (0.14 kg/capita/yr), 111th - fish (4.5 kg/capita/yr), 123rd - meat (9.9 kg/capita/yr), 128th - alcoholic beverages (2.3 kg/capita/yr), 129th - stimulants (0.17 kg/capita/yr), 132nd - vegetable oils (1.9 kg/capita/yr), 143rd - sugar (3.1 kg/capita/yr), 145th - milk (2.1 kg/capita/yr), 147th - fruits (5.0 kg/capita/yr).

The 1980s

Kcal supply in China was 2 358.2 kcal/capita/day in the 1980s, ranked 88th in the world, and was on a par with Saint Lucia (2 361.8 kcal/capita/day), Cabo Verde (2 352.2 kcal/capita/day), Madagascar (2 335.0 kcal/capita/day). Kcal supply in China was less than in the world (2 572.3 kcal/capita/day), and was greater than in Asia (2 333.4 kcal/capita/day). Structure of kcal supply: cereals (67.7%), starchy roots (8.2%), meat (6.6%), vegetable oils (4.2%), sugar (2.6%), and others (10.7%).

Protein supply in China was 59.8 g/capita/day in the 1980s, ranked 93rd in the world, and was on a par with Yemen (59.8 g/capita/day), Malaysia (59.7 g/capita/day), Panama (59.3 g/capita/day). Protein supply in China was less than in the world (69.1 g/capita/day), and was greater than in Asia (58.8 g/capita/day). Structure of protein supply: cereals (64.9%), meat (9.1%), vegetables (4.8%), pulses (3.8%), starchy roots (3.7%), and others (13.7%).

Fat supply in China was 41.2 g/capita/day in the 1980s, ranked 115th in the world, and was on a par with Eswatini (41.2 g/capita/day), Angola (41.0 g/capita/day). Fat supply in China was less than in the world (63.2 g/capita/day), and was less than in Asia (42.6 g/capita/day). Structure of fat supply: meat (35.8%), vegetable oils (26.9%), cereals (17.5%), eggs (2.8%), starchy roots (1.3%), and others (15.7%).

These are the levels of food consumption in the world rankings: 23rd - cereals (169.9 kg/capita/yr), 42nd - vegetables (76.2 kg/capita/yr), 49th - starchy roots (74.0 kg/capita/yr), 81st - eggs (4.0 kg/capita/yr), 90th - treenuts (0.22 kg/capita/yr), 95th - meat (17.5 kg/capita/yr), 98th - pulses (3.7 kg/capita/yr), 106th - fish (6.7 kg/capita/yr), 107th - spices (0.15 kg/capita/yr), 110th - alcoholic beverages (8.0 kg/capita/yr), 122nd - vegetable oils (4.1 kg/capita/yr), 123rd - stimulants (0.29 kg/capita/yr), 129th - sugar (6.3 kg/capita/yr), 144th - fruits (9.5 kg/capita/yr), 145th - milk (3.6 kg/capita/yr).

The 1990s

Kcal supply in China was 2 617.7 kcal/capita/day in the 1990s, ranked 77th in the world, and was on a par with Macedonia (2 620.4 kcal/capita/day), Trinidad and Tobago (2 614.8 kcal/capita/day), Uzbekistan (2 605.4 kcal/capita/day). Kcal supply in China was less than in the world (2 652.6 kcal/capita/day), and was greater than in Asia (2 494.1 kcal/capita/day). Structure of kcal supply: cereals (60.1%), meat (10.4%), starchy roots (6.4%), vegetable oils (5.3%), vegetables (3.6%), and others (14.2%).

Protein supply in China was 72.9 g/capita/day in the 1990s, ranked 77th in the world, and was on a par with Brazil (73.0 g/capita/day), Malaysia (72.7 g/capita/day), South Africa (73.4 g/capita/day). Protein supply in China was greater than in the world (72.1 g/capita/day), and was greater than in Asia (65.3 g/capita/day). Structure of protein supply: cereals (53.5%), meat (14.2%), vegetables (7.4%), fish (5.7%), eggs (4.8%), and others (14.4%).

Fat supply in China was 61.7 g/capita/day in the 1990s, ranked 99th in the world, and was on a par with Pakistan (61.9 g/capita/day), Northern Africa (61.5 g/capita/day), Senegal (62.0 g/capita/day). Fat supply in China was less than in the world (69.0 g/capita/day), and was greater than in Asia (54.3 g/capita/day). Structure of fat supply: meat (41%), vegetable oils (25.6%), cereals (11.7%), eggs (5.2%), vegetables (1.4%), and others (15.1%).

These are the levels of food consumption in the world rankings: 19th - vegetables (145.3 kg/capita/yr), 26th - eggs (11.1 kg/capita/yr), 30th - cereals (166.9 kg/capita/yr), 61st - fish (17.5 kg/capita/yr), 66th - starchy roots (67.1 kg/capita/yr), 86th - meat (32.6 kg/capita/yr), 100th - alcoholic beverages (18.7 kg/capita/yr), 119th - spices (0.21 kg/capita/yr), 124th - vegetable oils (5.8 kg/capita/yr), 140th - pulses (1.5 kg/capita/yr), 144th - fruits (27.3 kg/capita/yr), 147th - stimulants (0.34 kg/capita/yr), 148th - sugar (6.9 kg/capita/yr), 158th - milk (6.2 kg/capita/yr).

The 2000s

Kcal supply in China was 2 879.8 kcal/capita/day in the 2000s, ranked 65th in the world, and was on a par with Micronesia (2 884.7 kcal/capita/day), Kiribati (2 884.7 kcal/capita/day), French Polynesia (2 886.3 kcal/capita/day). Kcal supply in China was greater than in the world (2 765.9 kcal/capita/day), and was greater than in Asia (2 619.0 kcal/capita/day). Structure of kcal supply: cereals (51.2%), meat (13.5%), vegetables (6.4%), starchy roots (6%), vegetable oils (6%), and others (16.9%).

Protein supply in China was 87.0 g/capita/day in the 2000s, ranked 54th in the world, and was on a par with Brunei (87.0 g/capita/day), Saint Lucia (87.0 g/capita/day), Latvia (87.1 g/capita/day). Protein supply in China was greater than in the world (76.5 g/capita/day), and was greater than in Asia (70.9 g/capita/day). Structure of protein supply: cereals (41.2%), meat (17.9%), vegetables (11.8%), fish (7.4%), eggs (6%), and others (15.7%).

Fat supply in China was 81.5 g/capita/day in the 2000s, ranked 78th in the world, and was on a par with Central America (81.5 g/capita/day), Dominica (81.3 g/capita/day), Saint Kitts and Nevis (82.3 g/capita/day). Fat supply in China was greater than in the world (76.9 g/capita/day), and was greater than in Asia (64.4 g/capita/day). Structure of fat supply: meat (43.8%), vegetable oils (23.9%), cereals (8.2%), eggs (5.9%), milk (2.6%), and others (15.6%).

These are the levels of food consumption in the world rankings: 1st - vegetables (283.4 kg/capita/yr), 5th - eggs (16.6 kg/capita/yr), 42nd - fish (26.7 kg/capita/yr), 43rd - cereals (154.7 kg/capita/yr), 58th - starchy roots (73.6 kg/capita/yr), 76th - meat (48.5 kg/capita/yr), 85th - alcoholic beverages (31.6 kg/capita/yr), 87th - treenuts (1.2 kg/capita/yr), 112th - fruits (56.6 kg/capita/yr), 122nd - vegetable oils (7.1 kg/capita/yr), 128th - spices (0.21 kg/capita/yr), 144th - milk (20.0 kg/capita/yr), 150th - pulses (1.3 kg/capita/yr), 154th - stimulants (0.54 kg/capita/yr), 162nd - sugar (6.2 kg/capita/yr).

The 2010s

Kcal supply in China was 3 083.3 kcal/capita/day in the 2010s, ranked 55th in the world, and was on a par with Iran (3 075.8 kcal/capita/day), Mauritius (3 072.0 kcal/capita/day), Oman (3 098.3 kcal/capita/day). Kcal supply in China was greater than in the world (2 869.3 kcal/capita/day), and was greater than in Asia (2 759.8 kcal/capita/day). Structure of kcal supply: cereals (46.6%), meat (15.1%), vegetables (7.4%), vegetable oils (5.9%), starchy roots (5%), and others (20%).

Protein supply in China was 96.5 g/capita/day in the 2010s, ranked 41st in the world, and was on a par with Morocco (96.4 g/capita/day), Kazakhstan (96.7 g/capita/day), Belarus (96.3 g/capita/day). Protein supply in China was greater than in the world (80.6 g/capita/day), and was greater than in Asia (76.7 g/capita/day). Structure of protein supply: cereals (35.4%), meat (19.4%), vegetables (13.1%), fish (8.4%), eggs (6.1%), and others (17.6%).

Fat supply in China was 94.1 g/capita/day in the 2010s, ranked 60th in the world, and was on a par with Western Asia (94.0

g/capita/day), Eastern Asia (93.5 g/capita/day), Fiji (93.5 g/capita/day). Fat supply in China was greater than in the world (82.4 g/capita/day), and was greater than in Asia (72.1 g/capita/day). Structure of fat supply: meat (45.3%), vegetable oils (22%), cereals (6.6%), eggs (5.7%), milk (3.4%), and others (17%).

These are the levels of food consumption in the world rankings: 1st - vegetables (342.9 kg/capita/yr), 3rd - eggs (18.6 kg/capita/yr), 27th - fish (33.5 kg/capita/yr), 45th - cereals (151.1 kg/capita/yr), 58th - treenuts (2.5 kg/capita/yr), 60th - starchy roots (68.9 kg/capita/yr), 70th - meat (58.6 kg/capita/yr), 75th - alcoholic beverages (43.4 kg/capita/yr), 118th - spices (0.30 kg/capita/yr), 125th - vegetable oils (7.6 kg/capita/yr), 133rd - milk (31.7 kg/capita/yr), 140th - stimulants (1.1 kg/capita/yr), 145th - pulses (1.3 kg/capita/yr), 163rd - sugar (6.8 kg/capita/yr).

Part V. Reproduction

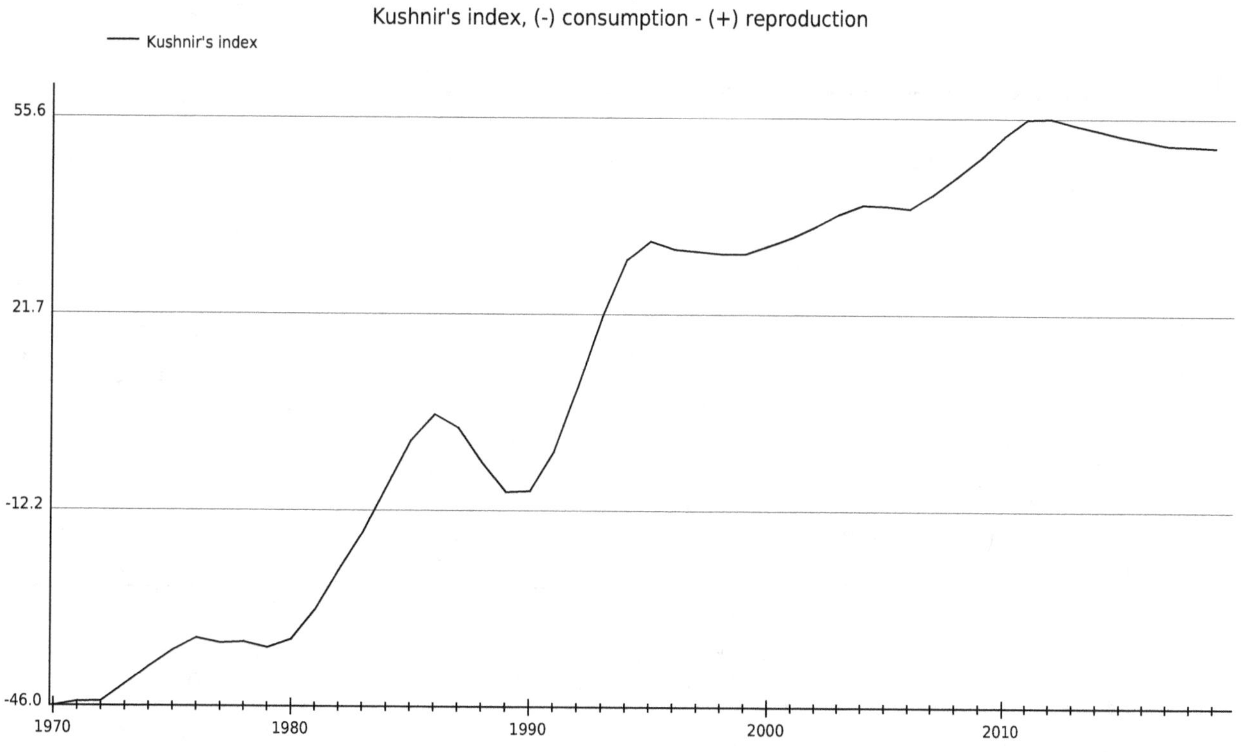

Chapter XV. Gross fixed capital formation

(including Acquisitions less disposals of valuables)

The fixed capital formation of China enlarged from $43.9 billion per year in the 1970s to $4.5 trillion per year in the 2010s, that is by $4.5 trillion or 103.0 times. The change occurred at $2.2 trillion due to a 1.9-fold increase in prices, as also at $2.3 trillion due to a 34.6-fold increase in per capita rate, as well as at $23.5 billion due to the growth in population. The average annual growth in fixed capital formation is 9.8%. The minimum value of gross fixed capital formation was in 1970 at $23.0 billion. The maximum value of gross fixed capital formation was in 2019 at $6.1 trillion.

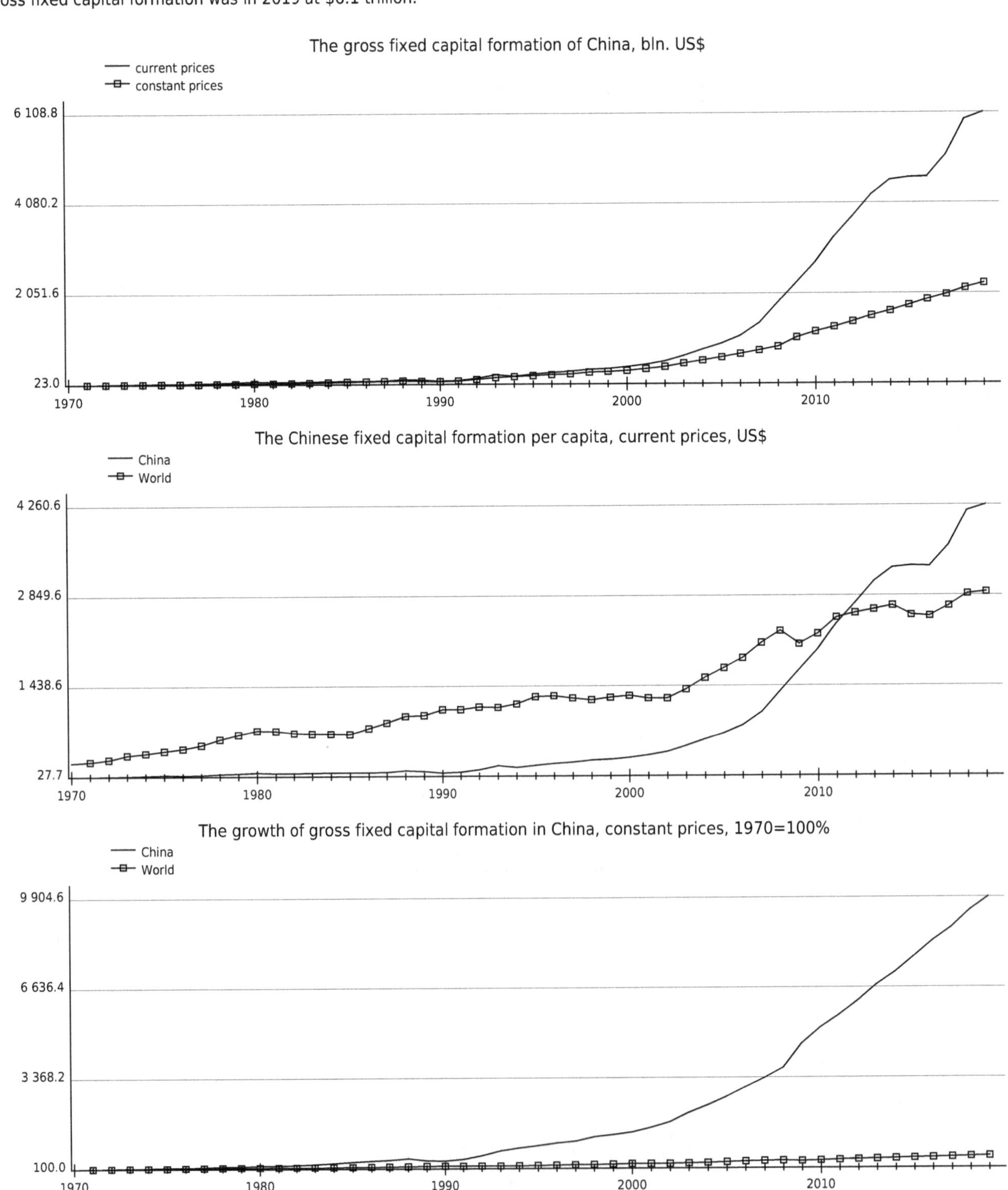

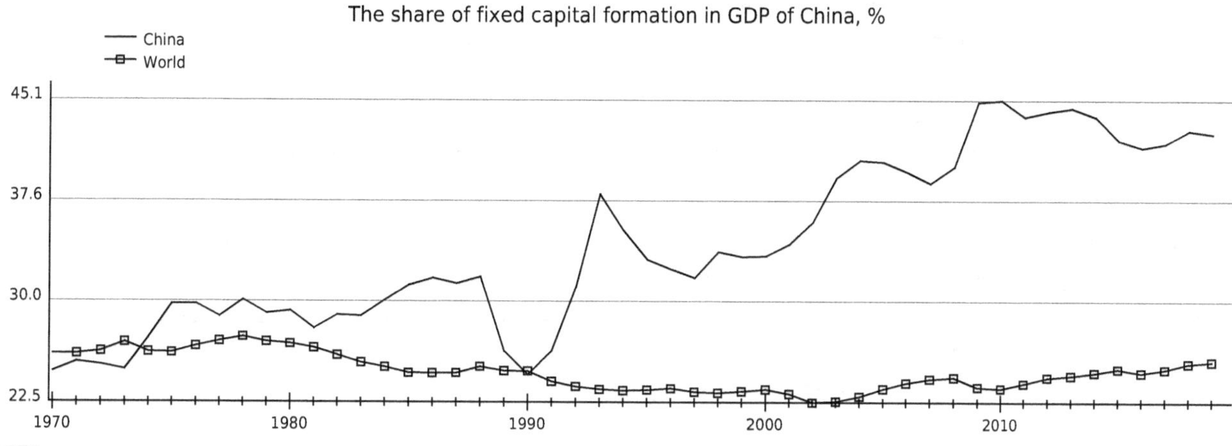

The 1970s

The Chinese fixed capital formation was $43.9 billion per year in the 1970s, ranked 9th in the world. The share in the world was 2.5%, and 12.5% in Asia.

The share of fixed capital formation in GDP of China was 28.1% in the 1970s, ranked 48th in the world, and was on a par with Portugal (28.1%), Austria (28.1%), Liberia (28.0%).

The gross fixed capital formation per capita in China was $48.0 in the 1970s, ranked 153rd in the world. The fixed capital formation per capita in China was less than fixed capital formation per capita in the world ($433.5) in 9.0 times, and was less than fixed capital formation per capita in Asia ($151.1) in 3.1 times.

The growth of fixed capital formation in China was 7.5% in the 1970s, ranked 68th in the world, and was on a par with Sri Lanka (7.5%). The growth of fixed capital formation in China (7.5%) was greater than growth of fixed capital formation in the world (4.2%), was greater than growth of fixed capital formation in Asia (6.2%).

Comparison with neighbors. The Chinese gross fixed capital formation was greater than in India ($18.0 billion), in Republic of Korea ($8.1 billion), in Vietnam ($542.8 million), and in Myanmar ($498.5 million); but less than in the USSR ($214.6 billion) and in Japan ($191.6 billion). The China's gross fixed capital formation per capita was greater than in India ($29.2), in Myanmar ($16.4), and in Vietnam ($11.3); but less than in Japan ($1 720.7), in the USSR ($850.9), and in South Korea ($232.4). The growth of fixed capital formation in China was greater than in India (4.7%), in Vietnam (4.7%), in Japan (3.9%), and in the USSR (3.2%); but less than in South Korea (17.7%) and in Myanmar (8.8%).

Comparison with leaders. The Chinese fixed capital formation was less than in the USA ($381.9 billion), in the USSR ($214.6 billion), in Japan ($191.6 billion), in Germany ($125.8 billion), and in France ($82.9 billion). The fixed capital formation per capita in China was less than in the USA ($1 750.0), in Japan ($1 720.7), in Germany ($1 597.2), in France ($1 545.4), and in the USSR ($850.9). The growth of gross fixed capital formation in China was greater than in the USA (4.4%), in Japan (3.9%), in the USSR (3.2%), in France (2.7%), and in Germany (1.5%).

The 1980s

The fixed capital formation of China was $98.1 billion per year in the 1980s, ranked 9th in the world. The share in the world was 2.6%, and 9.9% in Asia.

The share of gross fixed capital formation in GDP of China was 29.7% in the 1980s, ranked 34th in the world, and was on a par with Liechtenstein (29.6%), Eastern Europe (29.6%), the United Arab Emirates (29.5%).

The China's gross fixed capital formation per capita was $91.5 in the 1980s, ranked 145th in the world, and was on a par with Sri Lanka ($91.0). The fixed capital formation per capita in China was less than gross fixed capital formation per capita in the world ($790.9) in 8.6 times, and was less than fixed capital formation per capita in Asia ($349.2) in 3.8 times.

The growth of fixed capital formation in China was 7.5% in the 1980s, ranked 23rd in the world. The growth of fixed capital formation in China (7.5%) was greater than growth of fixed capital formation in the world (2.5%), was greater than growth of fixed capital formation in Asia (4.8%).

Comparison with neighbors. The Chinese gross fixed capital formation was greater than in India ($53.5 billion), in South Korea ($37.2 billion), in Myanmar ($942.9 million), and in Vietnam ($525.2 million); but less than in Japan ($571.7 billion) and in the USSR ($271.0 billion). The gross fixed capital formation per capita in China was greater than in India ($68.9), in Myanmar ($25.1), and in Vietnam ($8.7); but less than in Japan ($4.7 thousand), in the USSR ($984.8), and in Republic of Korea ($921.1). The growth of fixed capital formation in China was greater than in India (5.4%), in Japan (4.8%), in Vietnam (3.3%), in the USSR (1.7%), and in Myanmar (-0.40%); but less than in Republic of Korea (9.2%).

Comparison with leaders. The China's fixed capital formation was less than in the United States ($958.4 billion), in Japan ($571.7 billion), in the USSR ($271.0 billion), in Germany ($238.1 billion), and in France ($164.3 billion). The China's fixed capital formation per capita was less than in Japan ($4.7 thousand), in the United States ($4.0 thousand), in Germany ($3.1 thousand), in France ($2.9 thousand), and in the USSR ($984.8). The growth of fixed capital formation in China was greater than in Japan (4.8%), in the United States (3.1%), in France (2.4%), in the USSR (1.7%), and in Germany (1.4%).

The 1990s

The Chinese fixed capital formation was $233.7 billion per year in the 1990s, ranked 7th in the world, and was on a par with South America ($230.6 billion). The share in the world was 3.5%, and 10.2% in Asia.

The share of gross fixed capital formation in GDP of China was 32.6% in the 1990s, ranked 21st in the world.

The Chinese fixed capital formation per capita was $189.5 in the 1990s, ranked 150th in the world, and was on a par with the Comoros ($189.4), Mongolia ($189.3), Egypt ($194.0). The Chinese gross fixed capital formation per capita was less than fixed capital formation per capita in the world ($1 183.8) in 6.2 times, and was less than gross fixed capital formation per capita in Asia ($661.5) in 3.5 times.

The growth of gross fixed capital formation in China was 12.7% in the 1990s, ranked 12th in the world. The growth of fixed capital formation in China (12.7%) was greater than growth of fixed capital formation in the world (2.8%), was greater than growth of fixed capital formation in Asia (4.3%).

Comparison with neighbors. The China's gross fixed capital formation was greater than in Republic of Korea ($158.7 billion), in Russia ($98.2 billion), in India ($91.4 billion), in Kazakhstan ($5.7 billion), in Vietnam ($4.4 billion), and in Myanmar ($1.0 billion); but less than in Japan ($1.3 trillion). The China's fixed capital formation per capita was greater than in India ($95.7), in Vietnam ($59.4), and in Myanmar ($23.4); but less than in Japan ($10.4 thousand), in Republic of Korea ($3.5 thousand), in Russia ($664.1), and in Kazakhstan ($359.7). The growth of gross fixed capital formation in China was greater than in India (7.9%), in Republic of Korea (6.7%), in Japan (0.18%), in Kazakhstan (-17.4%), and in Russia (-17.9%); but less than in Vietnam (19.5%) and in Myanmar (13.7%).

Comparison with leaders. The Chinese fixed capital formation was less than in the United States ($1.6 trillion), in Japan ($1.3 trillion), in Germany ($520.7 billion), in France ($299.3 billion), and in the United Kingdom ($250.0 billion). The fixed capital formation per capita in China was less than in Japan ($10.4 thousand), in Germany ($6.5 thousand), in the USA ($6.1 thousand), in France ($5.0 thousand), and in the United Kingdom ($4.3 thousand). The growth of gross fixed capital formation in China was greater than in the USA (4.8%), in Germany (2.4%), in the UK (1.7%), in France (1.5%), and in Japan (0.18%).

The 2000s

The Chinese gross fixed capital formation was $1.0 trillion per year in the 2000s, ranked 3rd in the world. The share in the world was 9.4%, and 29.0% in Asia.

The share of fixed capital formation in GDP of China was 40.0% in the 2000s, ranked 7th in the world.

The Chinese gross fixed capital formation per capita was $782.2 in the 2000s, ranked 110th in the world, and was on a par with Serbia ($775.7), Algeria ($795.6). The gross fixed capital formation per capita in China was less than gross fixed capital formation per capita in the world ($1 690.7) in 2.2 times, and was less than gross fixed capital formation per capita in Asia ($905.5) by 13.6%.

The growth of gross fixed capital formation in China was 13.4% in the 2000s, ranked 17th in the world. The growth of gross fixed capital formation in China (13.4%) was greater than growth of fixed capital formation in the world (3.5%), was greater than growth of gross fixed capital formation in Asia (6.8%).

Comparison with neighbors. The China's fixed capital formation was greater than in India ($279.8 billion), in Republic of Korea ($258.3 billion), in Russia ($172.9 billion), in Vietnam ($19.1 billion), in Kazakhstan ($17.2 billion), and in Myanmar ($2.6 billion); but less than in Japan ($1.2 trillion). The China's fixed capital formation per capita was greater than in India ($245.8), in Vietnam ($228.6), and in Myanmar ($53.1); but less than in Japan ($9.0 thousand), in South Korea ($5.3 thousand), in Russia ($1 198.4), and in Kazakhstan ($1 119.2). The growth of fixed capital formation in China was greater than in Vietnam (11.1%), in Russia (10.0%), in India (9.5%), in Republic of Korea (4.1%), and in Japan (-2.0%); but less than in Myanmar (22.1%) and in Kazakhstan (15.2%).

Comparison with leaders. The Chinese gross fixed capital formation was greater than in Germany ($557.7 billion), in France ($463.9 billion), and in the UK ($407.2 billion); but less than in the United States ($2.8 trillion) and in Japan ($1.2 trillion). The fixed capital formation per capita in China was less than in the United States ($9.4 thousand), in Japan ($9.0 thousand), in France ($7.4 thousand), in Germany ($6.9 thousand), and in the UK ($6.7 thousand). The growth of gross fixed capital formation in China was greater than in France (1.6%), in the UK (0.66%), in the United States (0.43%), in Germany (-0.56%), and in Japan (-2.0%).

The 2010s

The fixed capital formation of China was $4.5 trillion per year in the 2010s, ranked 1st in the world. The share in the world was 23.5%, and 51.1% in Asia.

The share of gross fixed capital formation in GDP of China was 43.0% in the 2010s, ranked 5th in the world, and was on a par with Nauru (43.1%), Kiribati (42.9%).

The fixed capital formation per capita in China was $3 224.9 in the 2010s, ranked 67th in the world, and was on a par with Latvia ($3.2 thousand), Suriname ($3.2 thousand), Hungary ($3.2 thousand). The fixed capital formation per capita in China was greater than fixed capital formation per capita in the world ($2 621.1) by 23.0%, and was greater than fixed capital formation per capita in Asia ($2 007.4) by 60.6%.

The growth of fixed capital formation in China was 8% in the 2010s, ranked 30th in the world, and was on a par with Moldova (8.0%), Cambodia (8.0%), Iraq (8.0%). The growth of fixed capital formation in China (8.0%) was greater than growth of gross fixed capital formation in the world (4.1%), was greater than growth of gross fixed capital formation in Asia (6.0%).

Comparison with neighbors. The Chinese fixed capital formation was 3.7 times higher than in Japan ($1.2 trillion), 6.5 times higher than in India ($696.8 billion), 10.4 times higher than in Republic of Korea ($433.0 billion), 11.9 times higher than in Russia ($380.9 billion), 95.2 times higher than in Vietnam ($47.5 billion), 109.3 times higher than in Kazakhstan ($41.4 billion), and 222.5 times higher than in Myanmar ($20.3 billion). The fixed capital formation per capita in China was 22.6% higher than in Russia ($2.6 thousand), 35.8% higher than in Kazakhstan ($2.4 thousand), 6.0 times higher than in India ($535.2), 6.3 times higher than in Vietnam ($515.2), and 8.3 times higher than in Myanmar ($387.8); but 2.9 times lower than in Japan ($9.5 thousand) and 2.7 times lower than in South Korea ($8.6 thousand). The growth of fixed capital formation in China was greater than in Vietnam (7.4%), in India (5.8%), in Kazakhstan (5.6%), in Republic of Korea (2.9%), in Japan (1.8%), and in Russia (1.5%); but less than in Myanmar (10.5%).

Comparison with leaders. The fixed capital formation of China was 25.7% higher than in the USA ($3.6 trillion), 3.7 times higher than in Japan ($1.2 trillion), 6.0 times higher than in Germany ($752.5 billion), 6.5 times higher than in India ($696.8 billion), and 7.5 times higher than in France ($599.8 billion). The China's gross fixed capital formation per capita was 6.0 times higher than in India ($535.2); but 3.5 times lower than in the USA ($11.3 thousand), 2.9 times lower than in Japan ($9.5 thousand), 2.9 times lower than in Germany ($9.2 thousand), and 2.8 times lower than in France ($9.0 thousand). The growth of gross fixed capital formation in China was greater than in India (5.8%), in the United States (3.8%), in Germany (2.8%), in France (1.9%), and in Japan (1.8%).